My Bridges of Hope

Searching for Life and Love After Auschwitz

LIVIA BITTON-JACKSON

Simon Pulse
New York London Toronto Sydney Singapore

Dedicated to the State of Israel on the occasion of its Jubilee year and to the men and women—many in their teens—who lost their lives so that Israel may live.

First Simon Pulse edition March 2002
Text copyright © 1999 by Livia Bitton-Jackson
Simon Pulse
An imprint of Simon & Schuster Children's Publishing Division
1230 Avenue of the Americas, New York, New York 10020
All rights reserved including the right of reproduction
in whole or in part in any form.
Also available in a Simon & Schuster Books for Young Readers
hardcover edition
Book design by Lisa Vega
The text of this book is set in 12-point Garamond Number 3.
Printed in the United States of America
10 9 8 7 6 5 4 3 2 1

Library of Congress Cataloging-in-Publication Data
Jackson, Livia Bitton.
My bridges of hope : searching for life and love after Auschwitz / by
Livia Bitton-Jackson.
p. cm.
Sequel to: I have lived a thousand years.
Summary: In 1945, after surviving a harrowing year in Auschwitz,
fourteen-year-old Elli returns, along with her mother and brother,
to the family home, now part of Slovakia, where they try to find a
way to rebuild their shattered lives.
ISBN 0-689-82026-7
1. Jackson, Livia-Bitton—Childhood and youth—Juvenile literature.
2. Holocaust survivors—Slovakia—Biography—Juvenile literature.
3. Jewish teenagers—Slovakia—Biography—Juvenile literature.
[1. Jackson, Livia Bitton—Childhood and youth. 2. Holocaust
survivors. 3. Jews—Slovakia. 4. Women—Biography.] I. Title.
DS135.S55J33 1999 940.53'18'092—dc21 [B] 98-8046 CIP AC
ISBN 0-689-84898-6 (Pulse pbk.)

Acknowledgments

Without the dynamic encouragement of my agent, Toni Mendez, and the brilliant literary guidance of Jeanette Smith, this book would not have happened. Their friendship and enthusiasm served as vital ingredients in the magic of creation.

In addition to her superb editorial skills, which provided inspiration for excellence, my editor, Stephanie Owens Lurie, her assistant, Meredith Gillespie, and the rest of their team combined professionalism and humanity to create a remarkable circle of support.

I consider myself singularly fortunate in having worked in an atmosphere that made the writing of this book a labor of love.

Contents

Foreword

When I was thirteen, German soldiers bearing Nazi flags marched into Budapest, the capital of Hungary, and my life changed forever. Within days my family—my mother, my father, my brother, my aunt, and myself—were taken away from our home. We were delivered to another town where, along with thousands of other Jews, we were crowded into the synagogue compound designated as a "ghetto," or a transit camp, to await "deportation."

From there, a three-day ride in a dark, cramped cattle car with little air and no water was the prelude to our descent into the nightmare of Auschwitz, a concentration camp where close to four million people were mass murdered and a few thousand were kept alive to perform slave labor. My father was no longer with us. A few days before our incarceration in the train he was taken away abruptly, without a last good-bye, to a different forced labor camp.

Upon our arrival on the Auschwitz platform, my seventeen-year-old brother was shoved brutally into a line of men. Then a frenetic march of panicky women and crying children began. Driven by barking, ferocious bloodhounds and an ongoing hail of blows, the march ended at the gate of the camp. Here a man named Dr. Josef Mengele decided whether people would live or die. With stick in hand, Dr. Mengele selected Aunt Serena for the gas chamber together with the infirm, the elderly, and mothers with their children.

Because I was tall for my age and my blond braids made me look Aryan, Dr. Mengele, the "Angel of Death," pulled me and Mommy out of the line leading to the gas chamber. Instead of death in the crematorium, Mommy and I were condemned to life in the inferno.

Through a series of miraculous twists of fate, Mommy and I survived until the end of the war, a year later. On April 30, 1945, American soldiers liberated us from a train in which thirty thousand dying inmates from a number of camps were being shipped to an unknown destination.

By another one of those incredible twists of fate, my brother, Bubi, was put on the same train, and the three of us savored the bitter taste of freedom together. Together we confronted the reality of life after liberation—the full realization of our tragic losses.

Then we began the journey home.

Little did I know then what agonies and adventures awaited me, and that our journey to reach a safe haven would take six harrowing years. This book describes those years, the remainder of my teens, when we young survivors attempted to reclaim our lives while carrying the burden of the past. It is the story of our frantic search for love and meaning at a time when the world around us seemed to be collapsing under the aftershocks of the war.

This is the story of triumphs in the face of overwhelming odds, of extraordinary events in extraordinary times. And yet, I believe it is essentially the story of a teenager. It reflects the struggles, fears, and aspirations shared by many teenagers at any given time.

That teenager could have been you.

Homecoming

Šamorín, June–July 1945

We are home.

The farmer who gave us a ride in his cart deposits the three of us—my mother, brother, and myself—in front of our house, the family home from which we were deported over a year ago. The house still stands on the hill where it has been for half a century. It huddles in the shade of the ample acacia tree, just like before. But it is no longer sunny yellow. Its faded yellow is dappled by gray. And it has no windows. They have been removed from their hinges.

We were brutally wrenched from its bosom more than a year ago, and now, like a mad old woman, the house gapes at us, uncomprehending, unwelcoming.

The three of us approach our beloved house with bated breath. One by one we move through the cobweb of time, across the small courtyard into the large kitchen, the airy salon, the bedrooms. They are all bare . . . bereft of furniture, dishes, appliances, curtains, carpets. Even the water pump from the well is gone.

And there is a pile of human excrement in every room.

Our fondly remembered castle is a barren, debased skeleton. A vacant shell, divested of its soul.

Who did all this? Who robbed us of our home?

And where is Daddy?

"He must be staying with someone else," Mommy reassures us. "How could he live here?"

How can anyone live here?

"Straw!" Mommy exclaims brightly. "Let's get some straw from our neighbors. It will be fine. We can sleep on straw." Mother is back in her element.

Our neighbors, the Botlóses and the Plutzers across the street, and the Mérys down the block, are staggered when they see us. Are we ghosts having returned from the dead? They clutch their faces with both hands and shake their heads in disbelief. Alarm turns their exclamations into little shrieks of horror:

"Jesus Maria! Mrs. Friedmann?! Is that you?"

"Elli?! Can this be you?"

"Oh, sweet Jesus! This can't be young Mr. Friedmann!"

"You've come back! I can't believe it. We thought . . . we thought no one would come back from there!"

"Lord, how you've changed! I can barely recognize you!"

"How scrawny you are! I cannot believe this can be you!"

"What have they done to you?"

"Elli, what have they done to your hair, your beautiful hair? What's happened to your long braids? Why is it cropped so short?"

"Where's Mr. Friedmann?"

"Lady Serena? And the others? Where are they?"

"Has all the family returned?"

"Are they all so . . . skin and bones? So different?"

Mrs. Plutzer gives us a bundle of straw, a pitcher of milk, and a basket of eggs. Mrs. Méry brings a broom to sweep the floors. Mrs. Botlós carries bowls of fruit and vegetables. Mr. Botlós brings planks of wood and boards up the windows. Others bring sacks of potatoes, bushels of firewood, and the house comes to life.

Daddy will be surprised to see how quickly we made the house habitable. My brother Bubi's injured leg is sore, and Mommy urges him to rest on a bed of straw. Instead, he decides to go into town to find Daddy.

A number of young men and women have returned. Officially we are called "repatriates," deportees who have returned to their homeland. Some found their homes uninhabitable, and they are camping out in an abandoned building the government officially granted to the repatriates as shelter. But Daddy is not among them.

Bit by bit more survivors arrive. Daddy has not yet come. Where can he be? What is taking him so long?

We have been home for over two weeks when we finally receive news about Daddy. Some of the arrivals have seen him somewhere in Austria, making his way home in the company of a man named Weiss from a village fourteen kilometers from Šamorín. Thank God, in a day or two he will be home!

When another week passes in futile expectation of Daddy's arrival, Bubi hitches a ride in a cattle dealer's wagon to Mr. Weiss's village to inquire about Daddy. I want to go along, but Mommy worries about Russian soldiers roaming the countryside. We hear many rumors of rape and theft committed by our Soviet occupiers.

"Elli, this is too hazardous a journey for a girl," Mommy warns. "It's safer for you to stay home with me. Try to wait just a bit longer for news about Daddy. By evening Bubi will return. We will wait together, you and I."

An hour later Bubi walks into the house, his face deathly pale. As I stare at him, icy fingers stop the beating of my heart. In a barely audible tone Mommy asks: "Bubi, what happened?"

"I did not go. The cattle dealer gave me the news."

Time stands still. In the dead stillness the world begins to spin around me so rapidly that I must hold on to the back of Mommy's chair. From somewhere in the depth of the void Bubi's voice reaches me: "Daddy's not coming home. He died in Bergen-Belsen two weeks before liberation. . . ."

My scream is like the howling of a wounded beast. I run out of the house. Bubi comes after me and gently leads me back into the kitchen.

"Elli, I have to rend a tear in your dress," he says, and the sadness in his voice tears at my wound. "And then we'll sit *shiva* for an hour. That's the law. When news of death reaches the family beyond the thirty-day mourning period, they sit *shiva* only for an hour instead of a week. Daddy died in April, and now it's July."

I continue shrieking while Bubi's fingers rip into my dress at the collar, and his hands gently push me down on the floor next to Mommy. Mommy, her beautiful features white and lifeless like a china doll, sits frozen, staring into the vacuum.

How are we going to face the future without Daddy?

Back in School

Šamorín, September 1945

The long, hot summer days are over, and the leaves on our acacia tree have turned golden bronze. As I hurry down Main Street, clutching notebooks under my arm, I inhale the melancholy message of autumn deep into my lungs. The lingering aftermath of summer with its splashes of sunshine obscures a secret, bittersweet sense of passing. A canvas schoolbag Mommy made from remnants of a knapsack is proudly slung on my shoulder. I am back at school.

I am the only one among my fellow survivors who decided to go back to school, and now I am enrolled in my old school, Šamorín's public secondary school. I am back in the graduating class, in my old classroom. The smell of stale oil permeates the room just like before. The blackboard is cracked in the same places. The squeaking of chalk against the freshly washed board gives me goose bumps just like before. And the sudden buzz of the bell at the end of the session still has a startling quality.

And yet, not everything is the same. Different classmates. Different teachers. Different language of instruction. Our town and the entire region are no longer part of Hungary. They have become part of Czechoslovakia once again. Many of my Gentile friends and their parents, old Hungarian farming families and landowners, have been expelled to the other side of the Danube. New people were settled in their places. Czech and Slovak teachers came in place of the Hungarian teachers who had taught me. And whom I had loved. There is not a single familiar face in school.

Mrs. Kertész used to be my homeroom teacher. I thought of her longingly when I was in the camps, on work details, on endless roll calls, and in crowded cattle cars. In absence of pen and paper, I composed long letters to her in my mind, divulging my fears, my pain, and my panic. And I prayed that one day I would return and hand her all the letters, like chapters of my soul. In my mind I saw her smile and heard her praise.

I returned, but Mrs. Kertész is no longer here, and no one has even heard of her.

No one has even heard the name of Mr. Apostol, the former principal, who like a mighty citadel had towered above the school. Neither have they heard of Mr. Kállai, the popular science instructor, nor of Miss Aranka, the peculiar little spinster who made the teaching of math synonymous with terror. I am the only one who remembers them. And I have no one to share these memories with.

The time I spent away from here was not just a year and two months—it was an eternity. And the place where I was, the empire of death camps in Poland and Germany, belonged to another planet.

When I was taken away, I was an impetuous thirteen-year-old with long blond braids, brightly anticipating life's surprises. I returned a knowing, chastened adult, shorn of my braids and my bright anticipation.

My hair has begun to grow. And I have acquired two new friends. On the third day of school, Yuri and Marek approached me as I stood apart during recess and asked who I was. When I responded in Slovak, they literally jumped for joy. They did not expect me to understand them. Yuri is from the Soviet Union and speaks Russian; Marek is from Bohemia and he speaks Czech. Both languages are related to Slovak, and so we are able to communicate. All the other classmates speak only Hungarian, a language totally alien to Slovak. They are children of ethnic Slovaks born and educated in Hungary, and recently "repatriated" from there by the government. Having been born here, I am familiar with both Hungarian and Slovak. In a very short time my language skills have earned me instant popularity as the class interpreter. And of course, the friendship of Yuri and Marek. We have become virtually inseparable.

Although I have lost a year of school, my classmates are either my age or somewhat older. During the Hungarian occupation I took advantage of the option to enter secondary school after four years of elementary education. In Czechoslovakia and in the Soviet Union, five years of elementary are mandatory.

Part of me has trouble believing I am a student again, living in a world of classes, homework, teachers, classmates, and examinations, just like before. My school friends are concerned over math problems, Russian grammar, and Slovak composition, nothing else. How I wish I could be like them.

Two Russian soldiers pass, emitting little shrieks of approval. They certainly cannot be accused of indifference to girls, these Russians. One of them attempts to block my path, but I swerve around with practiced speed and continue my race down the street. All the storefronts are shuttered, although it's almost eight o'clock in the morning. Ever since the war the shops no longer open at eight. There is barely any merchandise, and many shops remain closed all day.

A huge Soviet flag with a brilliant red star flutters above the school entrance, partially obliterating the much smaller flag of red, white, and blue, the Czechoslovak colors. The school bell sounds just as I reach the wide front stairs. The front is deserted; all the pupils have gone inside. Oh, God, I must be very late. What time is it? I can't see the clock tower from here. Whatever happened to the eight o'clock chime of the church bells?

With suffocating tightness in my stomach I approach my classroom. The teacher looks questioningly toward the door as I enter the classroom. Pan Černik's rugged square face and soft blue eyes seem amused rather than annoyed as he nods acknowledgment of my arrival. The floor squeaks as I tiptoe to my seat in the last row and squeeze awkwardly past Yuri and Marek. Yuri always seems slightly embarrassed when I come late. He clears his throat with disapproval, and whispers under his breath: "Where's your assignment? I'll hand it in."

"Have you submitted yours?"

"Yes. He's already collected the assignments." Yuri snatches the sheet of paper from my hand and walks up to Mr. Černik's desk:

"*Pan učitel*. Teacher, sir. Friedmannova's assignment."

Pan Černik nods again with a hint of a smile and begins his lecture, Health Study. Although Slovak sounds are relatively new for me, Pan Černik's succinct pronunciation is easy to understand. He conducts the class with special consideration for the Hungarian-speaking students, pausing after every sentence, asking questions, explaining key points, and waiting patiently while we take notes. We have no textbooks, and every lecture has to be copied into our notebooks.

Before the war, there was a separate teacher for each subject. But now Mr. Černik teaches every subject, except Russian. He does not know Russian. A Slovak from the hill country in the north, he is a tall, rugged man, with wide shoulders and a kind, swarthy, tired face. Miss Drugova, the Russian teacher, is pert and plump, with light brown hair swept up in a bun. Comrade Drugova has a firm, no-nonsense approach to teaching. She makes no allowances for the humorous effect of Russian language peculiarities, such as her reference to Hitler as "Gitler," and to Hans as "Gans," and she considers the ensuing hilarity in class as a personal affront.

Comrade Drugova's eagerness to teach is matched by my eagerness to learn. I am like a musician in her orchestra, learning Russian with almost the same relentless tempo as Miss Drugova directs. Poems by Pushkin and

Lermontov, short stories by Gogol and Lazechnikov, plays by Chekhov. For me Comrade Alla Drugova's unrelenting, humorless blitz transforms the Russian class into a love feast of learning.

The Russian class has brought Yuri and me together. Our friendship has helped me learn Russian and Yuri practice his Slovak. His primary handicap was the script: Unlike the Slovaks, the Czechs, or the Hungarians, Yuri had to familiarize himself with Latin characters before he could take notes in class. Coming from distant Moscow, the adjustments in lifestyle were also much greater for him than for the Slovak nationals from neighboring Hungary, or for Czechs from indigenous Bohemia. I have sensed all along an invisible wall around Yuri created by the differences.

And I believe Yuri senses that while I relish the thrill of learning and the excitement of new friendships, in reality I belong to another world, a world far from the classroom. He knows that the gulf that separates me from my classmates cannot be bridged. Not by him. Not by any one of my new school friends.

The "Tattersall"

Šamorín, July 1945–July 1946

My secret world beyond the unbridgeable gulf is the Tattersall. The Tattersall is the communal home of our new family, our town's few survivors. Out of Šamorín's more than five hundred Jewish citizens, only thirty-six returned, mostly young men and women. Those who did not—our children, parents, grandparents, siblings, husbands, wives, aunts, uncles, cousins, friends, and lovers—have been replaced by an abyss.

This abyss is like a moat around the Tattersall. I am not sure who gave this bizarre appellation, the name of an English horse trader, to the abandoned building the authorities allocated for us "repatriates." The spacious house, with a cobblestoned courtyard, a large kitchen, and several sparsely furnished rooms, was abandoned by its owners, who fled from the advancing Soviet army. The town's leadership then designated it as a shelter and retreat. Here we created a niche for ourselves, an island of togetherness.

The world beyond the Tattersall belongs to "them," the former neighbors, friends, classmates, and colleagues who violently eliminated us from their ranks and robbed us of our loved ones, and our homes. The world beyond the abyss has lost its relevance for us. Our birthplace, the motherland that brutally expelled us from its womb, has lost its reality.

The Tattersall is our only tangible world. Here we are real: We have dreams of future happiness as young men and women, we have desires of emotional and physical fulfillment. The thirty-six of us spend our days in the Tattersall sharing those dreams. We talk as intimately as close family members, revealing our innermost fears, plans, and hopes. We talk about life far from here, far beyond the abyss.

I understand my Tattersall family's disapproval of my participation in the outside world. It is myself I do not understand. Why do I have such a passion for learning, such a compelling urge to reach out and touch that world? To be a teenager like other teenagers?

Miki is the only one who understands.

Miki is the secretary of the Tattersall, the most prestigious position in the family. He administers our food and monetary allocations from the government and serves as our representative to the authorities. Miki is tall and slim, with sloping shoulders and enormous light blue eyes shaded by drooping eyelids. I find drooping eyelids and shoulders romantic and exciting.

Miki approves of my returning to school and singles me out for attention during group discussions. He invariably turns in my direction and asks for my opinion in front of everyone: "And what do *you* think, Elli?" The others fix their eyes on me in surprise and patiently anticipate my stammered response, out of deference to Miki. Afterward Miki always strolls by my chair and inquires about my studies, his clear blue eyes locked onto mine.

Every afternoon at around 4:30 P.M. Miki has his tea in the dining room, where I do my homework. As 4:30 approaches I listen for his slow, nonchalant footsteps across the yard. I listen, and my heartbeat accelerates.

"Hello, Miki," I say softly, trying to control the tremor in my voice.

"Hello there. How's the work going? Need any help?"

"Well, it's algebra. But, do you have time?"

"I'm free for about an hour. Let's see, what's the problem?"

With his knowing, unhurried manner, Miki pulls a chair over, and within moments we are involved in the intricacies of algebra. A comrade on kitchen duty brings Miki his tea with lemon, a special privilege for the secretary of the Tattersall.

Miki's nearness does strange things to my senses. But I concentrate and drink in every word that escapes his lips. After the problem is solved and his teacup is empty, Miki takes leave with a nod and returns to his office near the entrance of the courtyard. I continue studying until the Tattersall gang begins to fill the hall for dinner.

Dinner is served at seven sharp. Miki always joins us several minutes late. I watch him from the corner of my eye, but Miki seems not to notice. Much before the dinner company breaks up, Miki slips out of the dining hall without a glance in my direction. Why is he so agonizingly distant?

But I know I will see him later. He will be waiting for me in his office, as he does every evening, to walk me home along Main Street, the entire length of our rural town.

I am the only one in my family who eats dinner at the Tattersall. My brother Bubi is away all week. Since the beginning of the school year, Bubi has been living in Bratislava, where he is enrolled in a preparatory course for the "matura," graduation from the gymnasium. It is a course designed for students who missed out on graduation because of the war. Before the war Bubi studied in Budapest, the Hungarian capital. But now that our area is once again part of Czechoslovakia and an unfriendly border separates us from Hungary, Bubi cannot return to his old school.

Mommy appears at the Tattersall occasionally only to socialize, not to eat. She is once again her old finicky self: She is unable to swallow food cooked by someone other than herself. She visualizes unwashed hands, unscrubbed vegetables, dirty utensils.

What a remarkable recovery Mommy has made! I cannot believe she is the same person who not so long ago made me swallow the repulsive, smelly mush doled out in Auschwitz. Mother would tease me when I convulsed with nausea at the sight of the bits of wood, slivers of glass, human hair, and even animal fur in the foul contents of the battered bowl. "Eat it, girls," she would cheerfully exhort us all. "Where else could you get such delicacy? Gourmet cooking, only in Auschwitz!" She would then put a spoonful into her mouth and swallow it. She would do this so we would follow her example and learn to consume the unimaginably revolting rubbish, and survive. Day after day she pleaded, threatened, and intimidated until we understood that no matter how putrid, how repulsive, how incredibly foul, it had to be swallowed, in order to live. Until starvation accomplished miracles. The mush was no longer smelly and repulsive; no longer was it difficult to swallow. We gulped it down with voracity, and in time we missed the solid bits that made the mess more substantial.

Once, several months after our return, I attempted to eat an unpeeled raw potato. A potato in the camps was synonymous with a dream. "Why haven't we ever eaten potatoes raw?" I had asked my mother one bitterly cold morning in the concentration camp when she'd managed to barter a bit of fabric she'd ripped off the bottom of her dress for a small, half-frozen potato. "It's so tasty. It must be sweeter than an apple." Now I scrubbed the potato and bit into it expectantly. It tasted starchy and cloying, and I was compelled to spit it out. How could my perceptions have been so totally overwhelmed by hunger? I know now what hunger can do, and I find the memory very frightening.

Back in her own home, Mommy is once again haunted by the specter of dirt. To my great consternation she succeeded in talking the Tattersall leadership into giving us raw foodstuffs in the place of meals, so she can prepare our food with her own well-scrubbed hands and utensils. I, however, have been reluctant to forego the fraternity of the Tattersall for the sake of fully guaranteed hygiene at home. So Mother and I worked out a compromise. I eat lunch at home with Mommy, join the gang in the Tattersall for the afternoon, and stay on for dinner.

Mommy is busy with her work as a seamstress. During the war, after the Hungarian authorities confiscated my father's business, Mother employed her sewing skills to help support the family. Now she is making dresses for the Russian soldier girls in exchange for supplies: a few eggs, a bag of flour, a bowl of sugar, a live chicken, a bar of soap, even glass for windowpanes. We have no money with which to buy these things. And even those who have money find it hard to obtain supplies: most stores are closed, or stripped of merchandise.

Shortly after our arrival in our barren home, Bubi came up with a lightbulb for the empty socket in our kitchen ceiling, and we delighted in the miracle of light. When Mommy asked him where he obtained it, he related how he saw a lamp on a night table in an abandoned house. Assuming there was a bulb in the lamp, he climbed through a window to find not only a bulb in the lamp but a Russian officer sleeping in the bed. Unperturbed, Bubi proceeded to unscrew the bulb from the lamp inches from the sleeping Russian's head.

"Wouldn't it be great to have light also in

the bedroom?" I ask rhetorically, fully aware of the impossibility of my dream. "Then we could read at night while we lie on our straw beds."

Half an hour later Bubi appears carrying a bedroom lamp. "Where did you get this?" Mommy asks in amazement.

"The Russian officer is still sleeping," my brother answers nonchalantly. "I climbed in and took the lamp from the night table. There are no light sockets in our bedroom. How could my little sister read without a lamp?"

Mommy is in shock. "My God, Bubi! You could have been killed. The Russian officer could have shot you! Please, don't do a thing like that again!"

"Of course not, Mommy," Bubi promises sheepishly. "We don't need another lamp."

The Russian personnel are well stocked with all kinds of goods. To prevent my brother from making any more hazardous forays for vital provisions, Mother hit on the idea of sewing for barter. She stopped a group of soldier girls on the street and, using me as an interpreter, offered to make "pretty" dresses for them. The very same afternoon a slew of young Russian women came to our house with the most stunning fabrics and ordered all kinds of apparel. I managed to explain that Mommy had no sewing machine. In less than an hour, two male Russian soldiers arrived hauling a battered old sewing machine into the kitchen, and Mommy embarked on a career of making fancy satin dresses, frilly lace blouses, and colorful ruffled skirts.

Since that day our kitchen has been brimming with *barishnas* and *tovarishes*, Russian soldier girls and their male counterparts. While they wait with enthusiasm and good humor for Mommy to put finishing touches on their garments, they sing Russian songs to the accompaniment of harmonicas and balalaikas. I love to practice the Russian I learn at school, and to sing along with these robust, good-natured young women and men. The local people despise the Russians, calling them primitive occupiers. I love them as heroes who helped defeat the Germans.

So I am not concerned about Mommy being home alone while I spend my afternoons and evenings in the Tattersall, waiting for a few precious moments with Miki.

Daddy's Coat

Šamorín, November 1945

Winter has arrived early. Frost covers the bare, spindly branches of our acacia tree, and everything shimmers in silvery white. The windowpanes that our Russian friends installed have grown translucent with the intricate white-on-white pattern painted by winter's artistic brush, and even the interior walls glitter with a crystallike patina. Only the kitchen window and walls are free of a frozen sheen. We cannot afford to heat the rooms. The pile of firewood Mr. Plutzer brought when we arrived must be saved for cooking.

My habit of racing to school proves an ideal solution for keeping warm. The coat I received in Augsburg has grown threadbare and provides little protection against the ferocious wind. Fortunately, the classrooms are heated, and by the time the first class is halfway over, the chill evaporates from my puffy joints. An American army doctor who examined me after the liberation told me I had arthritis and advised me to keep my limbs dry and warm during the winter.

I am lucky. I have a coat and sit in a warm classroom several hours every morning. But Mommy and Bubi have no winter coats. Bubi's rented room in Bratislava is not heated. He warms up at friends' homes where he does his studying. Mommy warms herself near the kitchen stove.

"We must find our winter coats," Mommy declares with determination. "We must get them back."

Before deportation, Mommy gave some of our best clothes and valuables to our closest Gentile neighbors for safekeeping. Nightly, during blackout, our Gentile neighbors would open their doors a crack for Mommy to slip in under the cover of darkness, carrying our things. Our Gentile neighbors risked their lives by hiding "Jewish things" in their attics and back rooms. It was an act of true courage and kindness to conceal "Jewish" garments, furs, blankets, embroidered tablecloths, and bedspreads.

And it was an act of kindness to give our things back to us when we returned. After all, we had disappeared without a trace. More than a year passed without a sign of life from us: Our Gentile neighbors were justified in believing us dead. They were justified in believing we would never return and our things would become theirs.

When they received news of our arrival, several neighbors hastened to bring back a number of essentials. Others did not volunteer to return any of our things; they feigned ignorance.

All at once Mommy remembers that she gave her fur-lined winter coat to Mrs. Fehér, and Daddy's to Mrs. Patócs for safekeeping.

"Thank God," she exclaims. "Now we all will have coats. You can share my coat, and Bubi will have Daddy's."

Mommy and I, a delegation of two, arrive at the gate of the Patócs's farmhouse to claim Daddy's fur-lined town coat. Mrs. Patócs is cordial, even friendly, but has difficulty remembering that Mommy gave her "anything at all" for safekeeping. As a matter of fact, she is quite emphatic in her denial.

Instead, Mrs. Patócs suggests names of other neighbors who "might harbor a Jewish treasure or two."

At the Fehér house, the scene repeats itself with a minor variation. Mrs. Fehér does remember Mommy's "lovely navy blue coat with the silver fox collar," but woefully informs us that all our things "were confiscated by those bastards, may Jesus forgive" her language. The "bastards" are the Soviet occupation forces.

In the severe cold Mommy and I shiver with bitter disappointment in Mrs. Fehér's doorway.

"Let's go to the Kemény house," Mommy suggests. "I remember that Serena gave them some things for safekeeping. Now that I am much thinner, I will be able to fit into my darling sister's fur-lined coat."

Mommy's older sister Serena was my favorite aunt. Her brutal separation from Mommy and me on arrival in Auschwitz, when she was sent to the gas chamber and we to work details, is one of my most painful memories.

Mrs. Kemény does not have any of "dear

Lady Serena's" things. And she does not know who does. She has no idea whom among her neighbors dear Lady Serena trusted with her "precious pieces."

"So, your dear sister did not return? Poor Lady Serena." Mrs. Kemény's sympathy is heartfelt. "Whatever happened to that dear, gentle soul? We were so close. So close. Dear Jesus, I miss her so."

Mommy thanks Mrs. Kemény for her kind sentiments and urges her to try to remember who might, after all, have Aunt Serena's winter coat. It's a bitterly cold winter, and the coat is badly needed. Mrs. Kemény is sympathetic. She is in deep thought, but cannot remember a thing.

While the two women talk, my gaze wanders restlessly about Mrs. Kemény's overstuffed parlor. Suddenly, the magnificent mahogany bureau against the wall catches my eye. I know this bureau. There is no mistake about it: It's Aunt Serena's!

I touch Mommy's shoulder.

"Mommy." There is a sudden silence, and both women stare at me in surprise. My voice bristles with a sense of urgency: I grasp

Mommy's hand and draw her in front of the familiar piece of furniture.

"Mommy, look at this bureau! Do you recognize it?"

Mommy stares in disbelief at the bureau facing her. She extends her hand slowly, tentatively to touch it. Then, gently, almost reverently, Mommy begins to caress the polished surface, and tears trickle down her cheeks.

Mrs. Kemény freezes as if struck by a thunderbolt.

I stare at Mommy's vacated chair and recognize Aunt Serena's dining room chair, part of the mahogany dining room set.

"And this, Mommy." As if in a trance, Mommy turns slowly and returns to the chair on which she had sat for almost an hour. She looks long and deep into the Gentile woman's face. Mommy's voice is very, very tired as she speaks: "Madam Kemény, how's this possible? How did you get my sister's things?"

Mrs. Kemény is silent.

"Tell me, please, Madam Kemény, do you have any other things that belonged to my sister? I'm not going to ask how you got them. All I'm asking is please return to us anything else you might have. We have no furniture. We have no warm clothes. Do you, Madam Kemény, happen to have my sister's winter coat?"

Mrs. Kemény is trembling visibly: "Madam Friedmann, will you denounce me to the authorities?"

"I have no interest in denouncing you," Mother says quietly. "All I want are my sister's things. Return everything, and it will not be held against you. We will never breathe a word to anyone."

That very evening, Mr. Kemény's horse-drawn cart delivers to our house the bureau, four mahogany dining room chairs, and Aunt Serena's kitchen table. And a large trunk full of Aunt Serena's clothes: dresses, skirts, blouses, underwear. And her fur-lined winter coat.

After unloading, Mr. Kemény hands Mommy a list of names. They are the names of Gentile neighbors who hold Aunt Serena's other belongings.

Mommy puts on Aunt Serena's winter coat, and once again tears well up in her eyes. I bury my face in the fur collar of my favorite aunt, who suffocated in the gas chamber in

Auschwitz, and the two of us howl with unendurable anguish.

The next day Mommy and I make the rounds of Aunt Serena's neighbors on Mr. Kemény's list, and we find among Aunt Serena's belongings two of Daddy's suits and several pieces of furniture that belonged to us.

In one of the bundles we find cotton thread, needles, and a pair of scissors. These things are unobtainable even if we had money. Mommy is overjoyed. She cuts up a fine thick army blanket we received from the Americans after liberation and sews winter coats for Bubi and me.

Bubi is unable to wear Daddy's suits. Although he is tall, Daddy's jackets hang pitifully on his shoulders, and the trousers overhang his feet. Daddy was forty-five years old and had a wide-shouldered, athletic build. Bubi is only seventeen and has very thin, narrow shoulders.

My brother the fashion plate refuses to wear the delightfully warm coat Mommy made for him. He prefers to shiver in the tattered old sweater one of his classmates in Bratislava gave him.

＊＊＊＊

Tonight I walk home alone and, as I pass the shuttered storefronts a short distance from my school building, a tall figure emerges from the shadows. Just like Daddy, he has an erect posture and walks with rapid, athletic grace. I increase my speed in order to draw closer. Just about two steps behind him, I can see the man is not like Daddy at all. He is shorter, sturdier. And yet, the similarity is breathtaking. In a sudden flash, I realize why. It's the man's coat, a short gray town coat with a high, opossum collar. I know it's a fur-lined coat. I even remember the name of the fur—nutria. I loved to cuddle up to the soft, silky lining of Daddy's town coat.

I quicken my pace in order to pass the man. Faster, faster. I must see his face. I must meet him face-to-face. I start to run, and pass him. When I reach a considerable stretch beyond the man, I swing around and walk toward him. I cannot make out the man's features in detail, but I see he has a square face under a wide-brimmed gray fedora.

"Hello, sir." I know I am being impetuous. I know I am taking a reckless chance. The man stops in his tracks. He seems startled. "Forgive me." Suddenly, I feel as if an invisible hand were strangling me. I can't breathe. It takes great effort to produce words: "I do not wish to be impertinent, but . . . I believe the coat you're wearing used to belong to my father."

God, what's going to happen next? What is the man going to do? Will he shout at me and order me to leave him alone, to get out of his sight? Will he become belligerent, threaten to call the police? Will he assault me?

The stranger stares at me, his face shielded by shadows. "Where is your father, *slečna*, young miss?"

"He is . . . he was killed. In a German death camp."

We stare at each other, and the silence seems interminable. "Yes. This coat could well have belonged to your father. I bought it about a month ago, not here, in another town. It's a fine coat." The man runs his right hand over his left sleeve. "A very fine coat."

A tremor passes down from my head and lodges in my calf muscles. My legs shake as the man continues to stare into my face. "How about the hat? Do you recognize the hat? I bought it at the same time. In the same store. Do you think it, too, belonged to your father?"

"I don't recognize the hat. But the coat . . . My father loved this coat."

We stand still, facing each other. Time stands still. People hurry past. Cold wind laps at my feet. The church bells begin to chime. It must be eight o'clock.

"Sir, I miss my father very much. . . ." My voice drowns in tears. "Please. May I have his coat?"

"Let's see. I live not far from here. If you come with me, I can put on another coat and give you this one right away. How about the hat, do you want the hat?"

"I don't know about the hat."

We walk rapidly against a fierce wind. The man halts in front of a two-story building. "Wait here, young lady," he says in a strangely cheerful tone. "I'll be back in a few minutes."

The man vanishes in the darkness of the courtyard. Will he indeed return with the coat? Will I hold Daddy's overcoat with the opossum collar and the soft nutria lining in my arms this very evening? Is this a dream?

A gate opens, and the stranger, now wearing another overcoat, emerges from the windy courtyard carrying Daddy's coat and the gray fedora. "Here, *slečna,* take it. It's yours."

"I'm not sure about the hat."

"Take the hat. It's my way of saying, forgive me. Forgive us, miss. For everything."

I clutch the coat tightly and close my eyes. Daddy. Daddy.

The stranger playfully pops the fedora on my head. "Here. It suits you better than me."

"Thank you. Sir, may I know your name?"

He shakes his head. "This is your father's coat, *slečna*. I am one of the nameless thousands who benefited from your loss."

He tips his hat and vanishes in the dark courtyard.

Miki

Šamorín, December 1945

One evening, when I am ready to go home from the Tattersall, I pause at the open door of Miki's office.

"Ah, Elli. You are leaving?"

"Yes, I have to get home."

"Wait. Let me close up."

Miki rises to his feet. After shuffling some papers on his desk, he turns the key in each desk drawer and slips each key into his pocket. Before turning off the light, he reaches for the large key ring on the wall.

He invariably fumbles with the keys, trying to decide which would accomplish the feat of closing the office door. I find it enchanting, his absentmindedness in never knowing which is the right key for which door.

We walk silently for the first few minutes. Then Miki begins to talk. He tells me that the British are refusing to allow Jewish refugees to enter Palestine—thousands of young Jews just like ourselves, survivors of ghettos and concentration camps, now languish in internment camps in Cyprus, and in refugee camps in the Allied Zones of Austria and Germany.

"But why? Why are they in prison camps now, after liberation?" I ask in shock. "The war is over. Germany was defeated. Aren't the British our friends? Weren't the Allies our liberators? Why would they keep survivors of German camps in their prisons?" My voice rises in indignation.

Miki attempts to calm me with the light touch of his hand on my shoulder. "Elli, please. You must lower your voice. Britain has been restricting Jewish immigration to Eretz Israel for years. They don't want any more Arab riots against Jewish settlements. Instead of controlling the rioters, the British gave in to their demands and limited the influx of Jewish pioneers."

The implications of what the British had done by closing the borders of Palestine at a time when the Jews of Europe needed a haven are unbearable for me. I had heard of ships filled with Jews trying in vain to reach Eretz Israel—they were turned back to Europe, where the passengers met their deaths. I never understood why. Now, with dread, I understand.

I am overwhelmed with what I have just learned. But Miki goes on, and my heart fills with wonder.

In tones so low that I have to strain my ears to catch every word, Miki tells me of a secret organization he is working for. It smuggles Jews across Europe, and then across the Mediterranean Sea on illegal ships, to Palestine.

Who founded this secret organization? I want to know. Miki tells me about an army of young Jews who fought against the Germans during the war. Members of this army, called the Jewish Brigade, now help refugees get to Palestine.

"Recently the organization had a secret meeting in Bratislava," Miki whispers. "Plans were formed to smuggle Jews out of Poland, Romania, and Hungary, into Czechoslovakia. The operation has begun. We've brought in large numbers. Members of the organization shelter them here until they can be slipped across the Austrian border."

"Here? They are here?" I ask, and Miki silences me with a touch on my arm.

"Careful. You must speak in low tones. Not here in Šamorín, of course. They are in Bratislava. Hidden in various places, until we smuggle them to Vienna."

"And from Vienna? Where do they go from there?"

"From Vienna the groups are led mostly on foot through the Austrian forests and across the mountains into either Italy or Yugoslavia, depending on which trails are open. In Italy, they board the illegal vessels under cover of darkness. . . ."

I cannot believe my ears. "Does the Tattersall gang know about any of this?"

"Not really. Some of the boys are involved. Information is passed on to them regularly, but they are not allowed to divulge it, even to sisters or brothers. It would be dangerous for the others to know. When the time comes for us to organize a transport here, we'll let them know."

"Thank you," I say, my throat tightening, "for trusting me."

Miki coughs in embarrassment. "I want you to know about the transports so that you can plan ahead," he says flatly, then falls silent. I look up into his face, but I can't read it. The street has turned completely dark.

"You can tell your mother," Miki continues after a long pause. "I know her. She can be trusted."

There is a long, awkward silence between us. I am finding it difficult to breathe. We reach the heavy oak gate in the back of our house. My hand trembles on the massive wrought-iron door handle.

"I'll let you know further details as they come in," Miki whispers and prepares to leave.

I don't want him to leave. Not yet. Not yet. There's so much I need to know.

"Does the organization have a name?"

Miki hesitates. "It's called *Briha*, the Flight, in Hebrew," he answers haltingly, his voice barely audible. He stands there, tall and slim against a pale half-moon, his blond hair like a wild halo about his head. Suddenly I think, perhaps all of this is Miki's wild imagination. Tomorrow morning in the Tattersall I'll meet the real Miki again, the careful, fumbling bureaucrat, the shy, silent introvert with the casual slump. Tomorrow morning all this will have dissipated like a mad dream.

"I'll let you know as soon as I get details of a new transport. My old friend Levi, a *shaliah*, an emissary from Palestine, is in charge of the office in Bratislava."

I must know more. I must prolong this moment of madness. "How is the operation carried out? I mean the crossing of the borders. That must be extremely difficult, and dangerous."

"Yes. There are *Briha* meeting points near the Polish border. The Polish border guards at these points are heavily bribed to look the other way when small groups of young people walk across and disappear into the forest. Sometimes the police in the border town have to be bribed as well. You see, transports are directed to the meeting points, but crossing is not always possible. Sometimes there are delays, and the transport has to lie low in the border town for days, even weeks. That's risky." He pauses for a moment, then continues.

"In these hiding places—we call them 'stores'—every group is given a slip of paper with a code number on it. And when the group moves to the crossing point, they must present it to the *Briha* leader awaiting them there. Only after the *Briha* man recognizes the number does he activate the chain of operations for the border crossing." Miki's voice takes on a strange quality of excitement. He speaks rapidly now.

"Once the transport is within the borders of Czechoslovakia, it's easier. Here we have a tacit understanding with the government not to interfere with our movements. The Czechoslovak government even helps us financially, together with UNRRA, the United Nations Relief and Rehabilitation Administration. They provide transportation and even some food supplies. Most of the food comes from the JDC, the Joint Distribution Committee, an American Jewish organization."

Miki draws closer. He bends down and continues in a slow, hesitant whisper: "We just received news about one of our ships. . . . It arrived in Eretz Israel last week. Although it arrived far offshore, on a moonless night, the British police found out about it . . . they must have been tipped off. They were waiting on the shore, a large military police convoy, and as the refugees waded ashore, they arrested them and took them to a detention camp near Atlit. In Eretz Israel. . . ." His voice trails off into silence. I hold my breath until he speaks again.

"After all they went through . . . to end up in a British prison. . . ."

"Is there no way to get them out?"

"We plan . . . something will be worked out."

What madness. "I still can't believe all this about the British. They fought the Nazis. They fought very bravely and liberated us from the concentration camps . . . they were my heroes, together with the Americans and the Russians."

"There are political reasons," Miki says simply, with finality.

I fall silent. Why is "political reasons" an acceptable answer?

"It's late, Elli. Good night." Miki reaches out and brushes my right cheek with his hand. His touch is like the moonbeam, fleeting, ethereal.

"Good night, Miki." As he disappears into the night, an overwhelming sense of the surreal envelops me. Quietly I tiptoe into the house, but Mommy is still awake. I cannot tell her about the transports, not yet. I have to think about the things Miki told me, somehow sort them out. Perhaps tomorrow. Or, perhaps during the weekend, when Bubi will be home. I hope it will be all right for Bubi to know. I must check with Miki tomorrow.

Tomorrow. Will Miki admit to all he's said to me tonight? Will I meet tomorrow the Miki of tonight?

A Letter from America

Šamorín, December 1945

When the war ended Daddy's younger
brother, who had emigrated to America years
ago, saw Daddy's name on a list of survivors
in one of New York's Jewish newspapers, and
he hastened to contact him by mail. And so,
in one of life's bitter ironies, it came about
that Uncle Abish's letter from America rejoic-
ing over Daddy's survival arrived shortly after
we received news of Daddy's tragic death. In
his letter Daddy's brother expressed concern
about our fate. "What has happened to your
wife? And to your children? If, God forbid,
you remain all alone, I invite you to come live
with me and my family in New York."

The painful task of having to inform
Daddy's brother about the newspaper's error
fell to Mommy, and she did so as gently as
possible.

Yesterday Uncle Abish's reply came. His

shock and grief, on top of his offer to take us into his New York home, deepened the pain of our mourning. In vain Daddy had planned for years to join his younger brother in America. In vain he waited for our turn on the U.S. emigration quota. Throughout the years of waiting he developed a poignant attachment to New York. With uncharacteristic pride he used to point at the staggering skyscrapers on postcards he received from his brother. "See?" he would say. "Over a hundred stories high. Can you imagine, a building over a hundred stories high? One day you'll stand at the foot of this skyscraper and experience the thrill of staring up to the very top, where it touches the clouds."

Oh, Daddy. Without you I don't want your impossible dream to become our reality. Without you I don't want to experience the thrill of standing at the foot of the skyscraper. Without you New York would forever be tinged with pain.

"Send me your vital statistics," Uncle Abish urged in his letter, "so that I may apply for an affidavit immediately."

Uncle Abish's letter energizes Mommy.

"Elli, you will take a course in dress design in Bratislava while we await our turn on the American quota," she cries enthusiastically. "In New York you and I will open a dress salon. You will design the dresses, and I will sew them!"

"And what about Bubi?" I ask.

"Bubi should continue his studies," Mommy answers with finality. I don't argue, and she goes on: "We will be successful in America, you'll see," Mommy promises. America is big and ambitious, and so are Mommy's plans. America will be our oyster!

How can I tell them, my mother and brother, that I am dreaming of going to Eretz Israel, not America? How can I tell them that ever since Miki spoke of the secret ships across the Mediterranean, Eretz Israel is all I can think of? How can I dash their hopes?

I keep my silence all weekend. Neither Mommy nor Bubi notices. In their excitement they are oblivious to anything beyond the America project. On Monday morning Bubi returns to school.

In the afternoon Mommy sits down at the kitchen table to write a letter to Uncle Abish, to provide our vital statistics for immigration papers. I know that I must break my silence.

"Mommy, I must speak to you."

Mommy raises her head, but her mind is still on the letter. "You wanted to say something?"

"Not just say something, Mommy. I must speak to you."

"Now? Right now? I've just started the letter to Uncle Abish."

"Yes."

She puts down the pen and absently moves over to make room for me on the wooden bench. But I prefer to stand. I position myself on the opposite side of the table and look straight into Mother's puzzled eyes.

"Mommy, I'm not going to America."

Mother's eyes widen, and her mouth opens a little.

"I want to go to Palestine . . . Eretz Israel."

"Palestine? Why Palestine?"

Before I can reply, she continues, her tone somewhat heated: "We have been making plans for America for a long time. We have been dreaming, Daddy was dreaming, about America for years. I believed you were excited about America."

"Yes, Mommy, the prospect of America was exciting. It was Daddy's dream, and it became our dream. But Daddy did not make it—he who wanted so badly to reach America. And I no longer want to go to America."

Mommy's silence is deafening.

I plead: "Palestine . . . Eretz Israel is part of us. That's where we belong. Mommy, you can see that, can't you?"

Mother's brilliant blue eyes search my face. "You're a strange girl, Elli," she says, and in her bafflement I detect a faint note of pride, a grudging admission of deference. "A very strange girl."

This is my cue to press on. "Mommy, Eretz Israel is our only home. The Jewish country is the only true home a Jew can have. After what happened to us here, in our birthplace, our fatherland, a Jew can never feel secure anywhere else. Eretz Israel is the only country where a Jew will not be a foreigner."

Mother shakes her head: "I don't understand you, Elli. We've talked and talked and talked about America. You've never said a word. You were eager and hopeful, just like me, just like Bubi. And now, when it's within our reach, you've suddenly changed your mind. With such finality. You have always been a strange child."

"You see, Mommy, last week Miki told me of secret transports to Palestine. And then I realized—I felt it in the pit of my stomach—going to America is wrong. After what's happened to us. After what happened to Daddy. For us there is only one place—Eretz Israel."

"Your brother has gone back to Bratislava. We cannot reach him till next week. Why didn't you speak up last night? At least we could've talked it over, the three of us."

"Oh, Mommy, believe me, we can be happy only in Eretz Israel."

Mommy picks up the sheet of paper and I can see the words "My dear Brother-in-Law, May God Keep You Till one Hundred And Twenty," the latter phrase in a Hebrew acronym. Slowly Mommy pulls the drawer of the kitchen table open, ever so slightly, and lets the white sheet slide through the narrow slit. "It can wait till next week." Then she rises to her feet, her face inscrutable.

"Let's heat up some potato soup."

Mommy puts the large white pot on the

stove and goes to the cellar to get some wood. I place a few sticks of kindling in the stove and light a crumpled piece of newspaper under them. The crackling of the fire is reassuring. Mother stirs the soup. I watch her without a word as she ladles the steaming liquid into two white enamel bowls, and my insides fill with a sense of painful longing.

We eat in silence. The warm soup courses through my body and stills my agony somewhat. Mommy has not rejected the idea of Eretz Israel outright. I believe my argument has made a dent in her American aspirations. Perhaps a truce has been reached. When Bubi comes home next weekend, the issue will be presented fairly, and the three of us will make a decision together. There is a basic condition, a nonnegotiable principle we had agreed upon shortly after liberation from the concentration camps: Wherever one goes, all will go.

The three of us shall never be separated again.

Destination America

Šamorín, January 1946

Since that magical evening a week ago when he revealed the secret of his work for *Briha* within the framework of Aliyah Bet, the "illegal" transports to Palestine, Miki smiles at me when our eyes meet over the dining room table. His gaze lingers, and I feel my face turn crimson. The others have begun noticing the change and stare at us in fascination. I am mortified, but Miki does not seem to care.

More and more often after his tea he spends time helping me with homework. Miki has opened a whole new universe of feeling for me. A thrilling new universe.

When Bubi comes home for the weekend and Mommy informs him of my sudden change of heart, my brother is flabbergasted.

"What made you change your mind?" he asks with consternation.

"It's Miki," Mommy interjects. "He's

working for Aliyah Bet. They have become fast friends, Miki and your little sister. He wants her to go with him to Palestine. Don't you think he's a little too old for her?"

"He's twenty-seven," I say quietly. "That's not too old." I am aware of the trembling in my voice. "I never said he wanted me to go with him. Miki has nothing to do with my decision. Mommy, don't you know how I feel about Eretz Israel?!"

Bubi listens with attention, and his eyes fill with sadness. "I knew about the transports," he replies with a deep sigh. "I was also thinking about them. For weeks I could think of nothing else. But then I realized, what would Mommy do in Palestine? Eretz Israel is for young people."

Mommy is silent. She knows that the severe spinal injury she suffered in Auschwitz prevents her from doing heavy physical work.

"What will Mommy do?" Bubi presses. "In Eretz Israel she cannot make a living sewing dresses. Who among the pioneers needs new dresses? Who among the pioneers can afford new dresses?"

The three of us carry on our discussion late

into the night. I can no longer present my case with my earlier passion. How can I jeopardize Mommy's health in the harsh conditions of Eretz Israel?

At the conclusion of the weekend the decision is final: We will go to America together.

Mommy and Bubi accept my resignation with sympathy, with concern. With pain.

The decision has changed our lives. Now we live on the emotional verge of departure. Letters to and from Uncle Abish, to the U.S. Embassy in Prague, to the Czechoslovak Passport Authority in Bratislava, and local clearances, permits, and applications are at the hub of our existence.

Secretly, selfishly, I am praying for a miracle that would bring Eretz Israel back into our agenda. After all, the documents have not yet arrived. Our passport application has not yet been approved. The U.S. visa has not been granted. We may end up in Palestine by default.

I keep postponing a confrontation with Miki. I don't want to jeopardize our relationship. Will his feelings change toward me when he finds out our family decision? Will he again become distant and aloof?

The Barishna

Šamorín, September 1945–April 1946

As it turned out, my relationship with Miki did change, but not because of our decision. The shift was caused by a rather unexpected turn of events.

About five months ago, right before the High Holidays, a tall, husky young woman in Soviet army uniform drifted into the Tattersall, looking for someone who spoke Russian. I was doing my homework in the dining hall when she came in, so I volunteered. As it was a month since the beginning of school and my exposure to Comrade Alla Drugova's teaching blitz, I had no trouble communicating in Russian. The *barishna*, meaning "soldier girl" in Russian, said she was Jewish and wanted to spend the holidays among Jews.

I became the *barishna*'s interpreter and mentor. The reluctance of the others to embrace her into the Tattersall family was caused less by the language barrier than by her robust temperament, which they considered somewhat aggressive.

She was a strange girl, the *barishna*. Her enormously fat legs bulged out of high boots into which they had been permanently compressed. She said it had been years since she had taken off her boots—she even slept in them. When I asked why, the *barishna* shrugged in reply. She said she was eighteen but looked much older. She also said she had been in the army for over three years, two of them on the front lines. We wondered: Had she been drafted into the army at the age of fifteen? We were skeptical, but it was pointless to ask questions, because the *barishna* was not in the habit of answering them. Even her name she did not divulge, so Barishna became her name.

Barishna was in the habit of lunging headlong into whatever interested her.

"That fellow Grossman you've introduced me to, he's rich, isn't he?" she asked me a few days after I introduced her to Miki, one of the few who spoke Russian.

"Why do you ask?"

"He must be very rich. You told me his family had owned a lot of land and houses. And he returned alone. So, he must have inherited it all. He must be a tycoon!" Barishna used the Russian word *bogach* for "tycoon."

I was taken aback by Barishna's reference to Miki's "wealth." I had thought her naive and childlike and even said as much to Miki, who was annoyed at Barishna's habit of joining us on our walks. I believed her behavior was that of an unspoiled innocent, and when Miki asked me to tell her to stop tagging along, I was reluctant to hurt her feelings. Now I was shocked when Barishna continued: "I think Grossman's the richest man here. He is heir to a bigger fortune than any of the others."

I could not understand what Barishna was saying. This kind of speaking was so alien to me that it was unintelligible. Had she spoken of "fortune"? Of "inheritance"? All of us were heirs to empty homesteads, fallow fields, businesses bereft of proprietors. Every survivor was heir to the agony of a staggering vacuum. How dared she speak of material fortune when we felt only the pain of our parents' tragic absence?

Barishna misunderstood my silence.

"He's rich, isn't he?" she went on. "Why don't you tell me the truth? You're his friend. You must know how much he owns. I saw his house. It's big. And then, when we passed the other big house, the white one on the corner, you said his uncle's family used to live there. And now it stands empty. The uncle's family was killed; nobody came back. So it's his. Grossman is very rich. You can't deny it."

"Why do you want to know?"

"Because I want to marry him. I *will* marry him."

"What? You will what?"

"Marry him. I want to stay here and marry a rich man."

She was surely insane. "He doesn't even know you. He's not yet spoken a single word to you." I did not tell her how annoyed Miki was about her intruding on our walks. He obviously did not relish her company.

Barishna was undaunted. "That doesn't matter. I want to marry a rich man and settle down. I like this town. My unit will pull out soon, and anyone who wants to stay, can. I want to stay here and marry Grossman. He will make a good husband, I can tell."

This was too ridiculous for words. But I went along with the farce: "Don't you want to go home and see your family in the Soviet Union?"

Barishna shrugged: "I don't know what became of them. The Germans killed everybody."

"Don't you want to find out what became of your family?"

"I told you, the Germans killed everybody."

"And how about him, Grossman? How will you get him to marry you?"

"I will ask him to. He will marry me."

"What if he says no? What will you do then?"

"I will ask him again, and again. Until he says yes. He will marry me." Then, with a conspiratorial intimacy, she lowered her voice: "You're my friend, so I tell you. I'll ask him soon, before a girl from this town gets to him first. He's rich; I must hurry."

The next day Miki greeted me with visible irritation: "Elli, I must speak to you." He motioned me to follow him to his office, then shut the door: "You won't believe what happened last night. I was awakened by loud knocking, and when I opened the door to see who the hell was making such a racket in the middle of the night, guess who was there? The Russian soldier, your protégée. She had a large, battered suitcase in her hand. 'I want to live here,' she said. I was so astonished, I just stood there, speechless. 'I'm moving in here right now,' she said, and started shoving the suitcase through the door. I told her sorry, but she couldn't move in, she had to leave immediately. She started crying and screaming about how heartless I was turning her away in the middle of the night, how she'd fought the Germans for three years and now had nowhere to go. Her unit deployed from the region, and all her comrades left. She said I was cruel to have so many houses and so many rooms and not even let her sleep in one of my rooms for one night. Tomorrow she'll go away. Tomorrow she'll find another place. What could I do under the circumstances? You've got to do something, Elli. She's sleeping in the back room. You must get her out of there. Let's hurry and get it over with."

I felt elated to be so intimately involved in Miki's life, to be called upon to help. I felt really grown up. We walked into the courtyard and headed for the small room in the back. When repeated knocks brought no response, he opened the door slowly, and we walked in. The bed was made, Barishna's clothes were neatly arranged on a shelf, and her suitcase was tucked under the bed. There was no mistake about it: The *barishna* had moved in.

Miki's face turned red. "What does she think she's doing? Elli, you must get her out of here. You must speak to her."

I promised to return in the evening. Barishna, however, was not there. The next day Miki greeted me with a look of exasperation. "She came back late at night, waking me with frightful banging at the gate. When I refused to let her in, she sobbed and wailed so loud, several neighbors opened their windows. It was embarrassing. I let her in for one more night but told her you'd be coming to speak to her. Please, go there now. She's expecting you."

Barishna was busily humming in the

kitchen when I got to Miki's house. "It's working!" she exclaimed when she saw me. "He cannot get rid of me. He tried but cannot. Isn't it wonderful? I'm staying here until he marries me. I've made it! Before any of the other girls. Soon we'll be married."

"Barishna," I said seriously, "Grossman asked me to tell you to leave. He knows we are friends, and that's why he asked me. He wants you to leave at once."

"Oh, that doesn't matter. He'll change his mind. I'm staying." No pathos. No hysterics. A simple statement of fact.

"Look, Barishna. You can't do things like this. In this country you can't stay where you're not invited. Grossman doesn't want you to live in his house. You can stay with us, my mother and me, until you find a place to live. Pack your things."

Barishna swung around and stared into my face. Her freckles stood out as sharp black dots on her round, pallid face: "Leave me alone! Just go away, I'm staying here. I like this house."

Miki was furious: "Tonight she's leaving whether she likes it or not."

The next day Miki waved his hand in a

gesture of resignation when I inquired about Barishna, and I did not ask him to elaborate. From then on Miki never referred to the matter, but it was common knowledge that Barishna lived in the Grossman house. Our walks ceased, and whenever we met, Miki averted his eyes. We barely greeted each other.

At first everyone was appalled, and criticized Barishna's conduct. But she ignored it all. In time snickering replaced collective outrage in the Tattersall, then indifference replaced the snickering. Miki-and-Barishna became an accepted fact.

Later in the spring rumor spread that Barishna was pregnant. A young Talmudic scholar was brought from Dunaszerdahely to perform the wedding ceremony. After the ceremony, Mr. and Mrs. Grossman left for Palestine.

How was it possible for this to happen? How was it possible for Barishna's selfish manipulation to succeed? How was it possible for immorality to be made holy through a religious ceremony?

And Miki. How could he? How could he?

Barishna and Miki both had committed an unforgivable breach against human ethics, and yet their act was socially endorsed, legally authorized. They were a married couple now, respected members of society, soon to become parents. Who would care to remember how this came to be?

Something terribly wrong happened, and no one seemed to care.

In my bitterness and confusion I lose interest in my schoolwork and my friends. Is this what jealousy feels like? Is this the taste of rejection? I feel my sense of loss comes from more than just the feeling of personal betrayal. My sense of reality has been violated. I want to comprehend life, people, relationships. I have been observing and learning and drawing conclusions about the secrets of love, sex, marriage. And now the set of concepts I constructed has collapsed.

I have hoped someone would say: "Look, Elli, what Miki and Barishna did was wrong. This is not the way things are. This is not the way the world is." But no one has. The rabbi married them, and the others shrugged, wished them good luck, and bon voyage. No one was outraged or hurt or even indignant.

Only I am losing weight in my anguish.

"I Cannot Bear the Sun!"

Šamorín, April 1946

I have grown very thin, and Mommy is worried about my health. She is convinced that I am harboring some dread disease, tuberculosis perhaps, a widespread legacy of the camps. After weeks of Mommy's nagging, I agree to see Dr. Tomašov, the local physician.

At the end of his examination Dr. Tomašov ceremoniously declares: "If you don't gain at least ten kilograms, you'll be dead before your sixteenth birthday."

Now Mommy's panic is justified. She launches a feeding campaign. Large bowls of bean or potato soup with *chipkelech,* bits of boiled dough; mounds of noodles topped with fried cabbage; enormous slices of bread smeared with chicken *schmaltz,* are daily obstacle courses I must tackle. I lack the appetite even to start the meal, let alone "finish every last bit on the plate," as Mommy warns.

Ever since last fall the girls and boys of the Tattersall family have started to marry, one by one, and set up their own homes. Most have married within the family and stayed in Šamorín. Others have married survivors from nearby towns and villages and left. In some cases new members are added to the Tattersall family through marriage.

Several members have found employment. Money has come back into style. And so has rivalry for material possessions. For bigger and better material possessions. The dark shadow of the past has not been converted into a guiding light for the future. What has happened to the lessons of the past?

The trauma of the Miki-Barishna episode has become a dark filter through which I perceive my world. Life flows from basic instinct, from urges demanding instant gratification. It moves in compulsive spurts, defying direction and meaning. There are no questions asked, and no answers given. There is only movement, mindless, haphazard. Life goes on simply because it is the immutable law of nature.

I am deeply troubled. Although Mommy's

communication with me has been reduced to "eat," "eat," "eat," I have actually grown thinner since Dr. Tomašov's dire oracle. In her despair, Mommy summons Bubi from Bratislava for a family consultation.

Bubi and I go for a long walk in the nearby woods, and I pour out my anguish about life's lack of meaning. About my fellow survivors' great betrayal: "They laugh and grow fat. They marry, and make money, and buy things. All they care about is new leather boots and leather jackets. All they dream about is a motorcycle. They are either owners of motorcycles or hope to be. They are either proud of what they own or envious of what the others own. They fall in love and care only about each other, forgetting about everyone else. Everything else. I do not understand. I cannot make sense of anything. . . .

"We have just lived through a thousand deaths. The deaths of little children, babies, beautiful cuddly babies . . . suffocating in gas . . . burned alive in open pits. . . . Our brothers and sisters . . . our friends, people we loved so, frozen to death on roadsides. Starved to death. Our darling aunt Serena gasping for air in the gas chamber . . . her gold teeth yanked out. Her skin pulled off to make lamp shades. Her meager fat made into soap. Her delicate bones made into fertilizer . . ."

I go on, and Bubi does not attempt to stop me.

"And we grow fat on potato soup and noo-dles. And make vulgar jokes and laugh. Dance at every wedding all night through. At every silly wedding we dance and sing and shriek with laughter. This hysterical merry-go-round of flirtation and courting and laughter . . . it's maddening. Maddening.

"We never talk about what has happened to us. Never. We keep staring into the sun and don't see the shadow. Frantically we keep turning our faces to the sun. . . .

"I cannot bear the sun! It's cruel. It's a hoax. Sunlight is mockery. So is music. I can-not bear the sound of music, loud and brash. It's deafening. I cannot bear all the food we are gulping down as if in a contest. It's nauseating. It's insanity. I cannot bear any of this. . . ."

I begin to weep, and Bubi walks by my side in silence. His voice is soft and somewhat hoarse when he speaks: "I understand your feelings, Elli. It's an understandable reaction to what has happened to us. I am very sorry you suffer so. You are very young. I believe you suffer so keenly because of your youth. You see, this thing you call 'merry-go-round' is a good thing. The search for marriage and money and the sun, this is life. They are lonely, these young survivors without parents, families. They need to find new relationships, reaffirm life. They must do this in order to keep from going insane, from being destroyed by memories. They must eat and dance and laugh in order to keep from crying. When one laughs hysterically, it is because one needs to cry hysterically.

"I know it seems abnormal, this rush into relationships, marriages. This constant reaching out for merriment. But can we be normal? Will we ever be normal?"

A wave of gratitude sweeps over me. My brother is so wise. He understands. Why haven't I seen all this? Although my anguish does not dissipate, Bubi's answer liberates me from the burden of my indictments, and I am grateful.

But what about him? He does not brood like me, and neither does he go into hysterical excesses like them. He lives a temperate life, is involved in studies, passes his exams, and enjoys the company of intelligent friends. His leg wound has almost completely healed, the scar on his forehead from his bullet wound has turned from red to pink, and the boils on his arms have disappeared without a trace. Have his emotional scars also healed?

Bubi stays in Šamorín for the night. Mommy cooks a festive meal—cheese blintzes—and enjoys watching his hearty appetite. Bubi's appetite was born in the camps. He used to be a poor eater. He used to be a thin, gangly boy. Now he is well built, tall, and striking, with wavy, dark blond hair. Before the war, like all yeshiva students, he had close-cropped hair, and earlocks tugged behind his ears.

"I think Elli should go away on summer vacation," Bubi says after dinner. "Children's camps are being organized, mostly in the Tatras. The mountain air would do her good. She would have appetite, gain weight. I'll see what can be arranged."

Mommy is delighted and presses Bubi to make inquiries about the summer camp immediately upon his return to Bratislava.

My First Job

On Wednesday morning Bubi unexpectedly appears, his face beaming triumphantly. I know that smile: It means good news.

"I've found the perfect vacation for you, Elli. A summer in the High Tatras," he announces in lieu of greeting as he walks through the kitchen door. "The fresh mountain air will do wonders for your health. It will improve your appetite, and you'll surely gain weight. . . ."

"Just a moment!" I rush up to him and put my arms about him. "Just a tiny moment, Mr. Magician. Please explain the magic trick. . . ."

"An organization in Bratislava is looking for an assistant counselor in a summer camp for homeless children in Vyšne Ružbachy. And I proposed you as a candidate for the job."

"You proposed me? But I have no qualifications."

"Let's say I stuck my neck out. I have some friends there, and they agreed to give you an interview. They're holding the interviews tomorrow."

"Tomorrow?!"

"Yes, all day, at their headquarters at the Svoradova Street Seminary. I came to take you back with me this afternoon. You can spend the night at my place and be the first applicant to be interviewed, bright and early in the morning."

"But . . . what qualifications does a counselor have to have?"

"Don't ask so many questions. Pack your things. We have to catch the one P.M. train so I can make my evening class."

Mommy helps me pack, agog with excitement. She also packs sandwiches and a bag of *pogácsa,* her very special, firm butter pastries. She accompanies us to the train and, as the train pulls out of the station, she waves to me, her face lit up by a brilliant, sunny smile I have not seen for a long time.

The trip to Bratislava is an unexpected treat. The thrill of going to the city in the company of my big brother compensates for my initial panic at the thought of the interview. And for a feeling of guilt about missing school tomorrow.

Thursday morning Bubi walks with me to the corner of Svoradova, where he takes a tram to his school. *"Hazak Ve'Ematz!"* he shouts as he hops onto the streetcar. "Be strong and of good courage," the Zionist greeting in Hebrew, does little for my spirits. I climb the hilly slope of Svoradova Street with trepidation. I have no experience. I have never been a children's counselor before, or a baby-sitter. I know nothing about children. I have had no younger brothers or sisters. Not even younger cousins. And I had never played with my friends' younger siblings.

Svoradova 7, a girls' seminary, is a rambling three-story building with a flight of stairs leading to a side entrance. In the entrance hall flocks of girls seemingly my age pass me, busily chatting and ignoring my attempts to inquire about the director's office. Finally one of them pauses long enough to point to the stairwell leading to the second floor.

Three women and a man turn their faces to

the door as I enter. They nod in unison when I introduce myself. Then all four glance at their watches in surprise when I apologize for being late. I blush—I am not late at all. It is simply force of habit. Or is it nerves?

First the interviewers take turns in describing my duties. I find out that the girls' camp consists of twenty girls ranging in ages from four to sixteen. A counselor is expected to serve as mother, caretaker, and teacher to these children, most of whom do not even remember their parents. The counselor has to provide love, security, education, and discipline.

After the general introduction of the counselor's duties, a member of the panel hands me the outline of studies for the summer. The assistant counselor's task is to conduct classes for the younger children and supervise the homework activities of the older ones.

"These youngsters lost years of schooling," she explains. "And it is the objective of our organization to provide them with the basics of Jewish education."

I look at the study outline, and a wave of dizziness washes over me. I cannot even read the headings of the daily program, which are in Hebrew script. My own Jewish education has been practically nonexistent. I can recognize only the printed letters of the Hebrew alphabet. I have been taught to read printed Hebrew characters in order to recite the prayers in the prayer book. I have done this all my life without understanding the words I am reciting.

I know neither ancient nor modern Jewish history. I am familiar neither with biblical nor with modern Hebrew literature. I have been taught to observe Jewish law without knowing the reasons underlying the various rituals.

I have no choice but to admit the truth about my lack of Jewish educational background. I also reveal to the panel that I have had no experience with children of any age.

"I apologize for having wasted the committee's time," I say in conclusion to my list of confessions. The panel accepts my apology, nodding in unison once again. The chairperson, a short, slim woman of about thirty with straight, shiny black hair, promises to notify my brother of the panel's decision.

For me, the polite, formal handshakes at the end of the interview suffice as notification—I know I have lost the job. I am disappointed about missing the summer vacation, yet, strangely, instead of sadness I am filled with a sense of elation. I have come across something wonderful on the baffling pages of the study outline. I have discovered a new world I did not know existed. I have found a niche of relevance. I have found myself; I know I belong to that niche.

It is this sense of elation that carries me downhill on Svoradova Street toward the Carlton Hotel, where I am to meet my brother. I have made a decision. I am going to enroll in the Seminary to study Judaism. As if I had broken through a wall of isolation, all of a sudden I feel free. I feel free to reach out for life. And life, magically, assumes meaning. Breathless with anticipation, I hurry to meet my brother.

Bubi is sitting on a bench on Carlton Square facing the Danube. As I approach him, his face takes on a look of happy surprise: "How did it go? What job have they assigned to you?"

"I didn't get the job. But I don't mind. I know I don't qualify. Bubi, I've just discovered I don't know a thing. Zero."

Bubi is startled. "Is that what makes you so happy?"

"You don't understand. The study guidelines the committee gave me—Bubi, I've never seen anything like them. Bible, Jewish ethics, history, Hebrew language, literature. Everything. Bubi, I never knew how ignorant I was! It's absolutely appalling. I couldn't even read the headings of the study guideline. Bubi, I want to enroll in the Seminary. I want to learn everything. Will you help me get in? I want to enroll for this fall."

"Okay. But what about the job? What makes you think you didn't get it? Did they tell you?"

"I told you, I don't know a thing. I simply don't qualify. They will have classes in Jewish studies every morning, and the assistant counselor is supposed to teach the younger children. How can I teach if I don't know a thing? In the afternoon the counselors are supposed to lead the children in group games. I don't know any group games. I've never belonged to a group that played games. They also said the counselors have to be substitute mothers. I don't know how to be a substitute mother. I've never had anything to do with little children. I am simply not cut out for this job."

Suddenly a heavy blanket of clouds conceals the sun, and a cold wind ruffles my thin, plaid skirt. The metal park bench feels like a sheet of ice.

"It's getting cold. Come, I will take you to the station."

Bubi carries my canvas bag as we walk down Michalovska Street to the Manderla Building, where we will catch a streetcar to the train station.

"About the job—they have no way of knowing about your lack of background. Or your lack of experience with children. Did you tell them your age?"

"They did not ask my age. By the way, some of the children are sixteen, that's older than me. But I had to tell them about the lack of my Jewish education. My ignorance is obvious. And how could I not admit my lack of experience with little children?"

"According to Dr. Tomašov, it's imperative that you gain weight. The Tatras are ideal for that. They have sanatoriums in the Tatras for people like you. You must get to the Tatras somehow. I think you can tackle the job. I know Frieda Gelber, the counselor. She will teach you. And you'll learn fast. You'll see."

There is no point in arguing with Bubi. I don't mind being rejected. I do not want to undertake a job I know I am not qualified for.

Mommy is bitterly disappointed by the news. And worried. She is also convinced my health depends on this vacation in the Tatras.

Bubi comes home for the Sabbath, his face beaming once again. He turns to Mommy, for additional effect.

"Elli got the job as assistant counselor! They'll train her. In about two weeks she'll have to return to the Seminary, for a day or two, to be trained for the job."

"Bubi! How did you do it?"

"The committee said they appreciated your honesty," Bubi declares with mock solemnity. "And they felt you were *mature* enough to handle the task. And *intelligent* enough to learn. Mature! And intelligent!" My big brother emphasizes the adjectives with a chuckle. "I listened politely and, for the sake of your health, I let wisdom prevail and withheld my views on the subject."

Mommy is delighted. "You'll need a warm sweater. I found rolls of wool thread in the rubbish in the attic, a nice rich brown color. I will start knitting right away so that it is ready before you leave." She turns to Bubi: "When does the camp begin?"

"The first week in July," Bubi answers. "She'll also need warm pajamas. Nights are very cold high up there. It's a ten-hour journey by train to Vyšne Ružbachy, and from there another two hours by carriage to the villas that will serve as summer camp. One villa for the girls' and the other for the boys' camp."

I can barely contain my excitement. A ten-hour train ride, and then a long carriage ride into the mountains! The fabulous mountains I have heard so much about but never dreamed I'd see.

Will I live up to everyone's expectations? Am I mature enough?

I Am Going on Vacation

Mommy accompanies me to the train station and helps me lug the canvas bag containing my wardrobe. I own a beautiful silk dress that came in a CARE package from America. When it arrived Mommy at first admired the lovely dress, but then she spotted a large cigarette burn on the skirt. "Look!" Mommy exclaimed. "What a shame! Right up front, in the most noticeable spot!"

"What luck," I retorted. "Without that cigarette burn the owner never would have put this dress in a CARE package. Thanks to that cigarette burn, I have a lovely silk dress."

Mommy laughed and immediately set about concealing the hole in a neat fold.

My canvas bag also contains a pink outfit made from bed linen that arrived in the same CARE package. Pink sheets and pillowcases!

All our neighbors were agog with amazement when it arrived. No one had ever seen bed linen other than white. What will the Americans think of next? Mommy turned the sheet into a full peasant skirt, and the pillowcase into a matching bolero jacket, the fashion rage of the time.

I am wearing a red-and-white-print jumper and a white blouse Bubi found in an abandoned villa in Seeshaupt several weeks after our liberation in that Bavarian town. The outfit must have belonged to a large woman: Both the jumper and the blouse were enormous, but Mommy adjusted them to fit my figure. I look elegant and cheerful in the outfit; the billowing puffed sleeves of the blouse make me look grown up.

Mommy's creative mastery with leftover fabrics is stupefying. The *barishnas* often bring much more material than Mommy needs to make their dresses, and then refuse to take away the leftover pieces of fabric. From these Mommy has produced an entire wardrobe for me and for herself. She has even sewn trousers for Bubi from gabardine left over from pleated skirts, a great favorite of the *barishnas*.

The conductor's whistle blows. Mommy and I embrace, and I hop onto the lowest rung of the train. All at once, Mommy's voice breaks: "Take good care of yourself, Elli. Be a counselor to yourself, too. Remember, you, too, are still a child. . . ."

"Oh, Mommy." A quick wave of the hand, and the train jerks into motion. My throat tightens. Oh, God. The train picks up speed, and the rapidly increasing distance between Mommy and me suddenly contracts my stomach into a tiny ball. Will I ever see Mommy again? Oh, God. I should not leave her. The train races on, and Mommy recedes into a blur.

The train compartment is stifling. Sweat covers my face, arms, hands. I need air. In vain I yank at the window latch: It does not give.

"Is anything the matter, miss?" the conductor inquires.

"My window is jammed. Can you open it, please?"

With a quick tug the conductor opens the window, and a gust of air slaps against my face. "Oh, thank you." The conductor nods and moves on. I take a deep breath and settle into my seat. Bit by bit my panic subsides as I watch the familiar scenery, the flat green plain, clumps of oak and acacia, and an endless row of telephone poles whiz by. This is the first separation. I'll be gone for nearly two months. The time will pass, and I will return to find Mommy alive and well. There is nothing to fear.

My thoughts drift to the High Tatras. They defy my imagination. I keep thinking of these fabulous mountains, but I cannot picture them. I keep thinking of cool summer nights, yet I cannot conceive of having to wear warm pajamas. In Šamorín most summer nights are blistering. The town is nestled between the Danube River and the Carpathian foothills and collects hot air like a basin, often turning my bedroom into a sweltering sauna.

My anticipation of a vacation in the High Tatras overshadowed even the prospect of graduation, and the day arrived all too quickly.

Pan Černik, decked out in a crumpled dark blue suit and a bow tie, handed each of us a diploma with great formality. After shaking each pupil's hand, he bade us farewell with the weary yet warm smile we had come to know and love. In a mist of nostalgia we parted with fervent promises of keeping in touch.

Most of my classmates made plans to meet during the summer at the banks of the Danube, but not Yuri, Marek, or me. Yuri was going to Moscow to visit his grandparents, and Marek's family was going to spend the summer on a farm near Prague. I was considered the luckiest—summer vacation in the Tatras was everyone's wildest dream.

All of us classmates left the school building together. At every street corner, as one or two broke away from the group, there were new farewells, new promises of reunion. As we neared the lower end of Main Street, Yuri and I found ourselves alone. He accompanied me all the way home, and we talked about his forthcoming trip to Moscow, my anticipation of the Tatras, the teachers and the school we had already started to miss. But all along, a question, like a ghost, was lurking in our dialogue.

We reached my heavy brown oak gate and lingered in front of my house, making small talk. Finally Yuri's question materialized: "Do you remember our walk to the Danube last February?" he asked. His voice was as taut as the string of a violin.

"Yes."

"You said then that you had decided to leave Czechoslovakia. Is your decision final?"

"Yes, Yuri. It's final."

"I thought perhaps you'd changed your mind since then."

"No, Yuri, I haven't. Actually, it's not only my decision. My mother, my brother, and I made the decision together."

"Do you know where you're going?"

"I guess America. My brother wants to go to America, and my mother doesn't want us to separate. I want to go to Palestine. But I don't want to part from my mother and brother, either. So, we submitted applications to the American Embassy."

"Will you be here when I get back from Moscow?"

"In the fall? Sure. These things take time. Except . . . I will be in Bratislava, at a girls' seminary. But I will be home for weekends."

Yuri's handshake was almost as firm as Pan Černik's. With a pang I realized how much I would miss him. Even the thought of the Tatras did not allay the sudden twinge. A residue of ache persisted for days. For Yuri, Marek, Pan Černik, and all the others. Because I knew the separation was forever.

An hour later the city lights pop into view, and the train slows on its approach to Bratislava's Main Terminal. Bubi's embrace is warmer than usual. How did he guess that I need his warmth, his reassurance, tonight more than ever?

Bubi lives in a small apartment in Bratislava which he shares with a roommate named Max. I met Max when I spent the night in Bubi's room before my interview. He is perhaps only a few years older than my brother, but his large black-rimmed glasses make him look very mature and intelligent. Although he is shorter and slimmer than my brother, he projects an aura of authority I find very impressive. Despite their differences in age and temperament, Bubi and Max get along famously. Both have a keen sense of humor and fun, and enjoy great popularity among fellow students of both sexes. The apartment is always bustling with company.

I am looking forward to spending the night there again prior to my departure for the Tatras so as to be ready to join the group bright and early. For me it is a special treat to be part of my brother's friends' lively company, if only for a rare evening. Especially in the company of Max.

During my last visit Max said my hair was of striking color and texture, and he liked the way I wore it, long with soft waves "cascading" to my shoulders. Since our return from the camps I have not had a haircut, and luckily the last throes of a permanent left traces of a wave in my otherwise very straight hair. Max also remarked that it was a shame the doctor ordered I gain ten kilo. "Your figure is just right as it is," he said with a meaningful wink that made me blush.

Max's compliments have made me conscious of my appearance. I have taken to brushing my hair and watching my figure in the long mirror we recently recovered from a neighboring farm. A leafy design carved into each corner of the mirror helped me recognize it in the parlor of the farmhouse where I went to buy eggs. While the farmer's wife placed the eggs one by one into my basket, I stared at the mirror in shock. When she finished counting, I said to her, "Mrs. Szantos, this is our mirror. I recognize the design in the corners."

The farmer's wife shrugged and said, "If it's yours, it's yours. I can't help it." The next day I borrowed a bicycle and rode to the farmhouse. The farmer's wife helped me tie the mirror to the backseat, and I walked with the bicycle and the mirror all the way from the farm to our house, two and a half kilometers. Mommy could not believe her eyes. She, too, recognized the mirror instantly, and tears sprang into her eyes.

I have spent hours before the mirror, simply gazing at my face, my hair, my figure. I am fifteen and a half, and my body is growing into the body of a woman. Max was the first person to notice it. With ten kilo gained I will look much better. Even Max will approve. No one likes thin women. In the summer camp I will force myself to eat, and fill out.

Mommy is happy that I have "rediscovered" the mirror. Besides my thinness, she worries about my concentration on studies to the exclusion of everything else. She worries about my lack of interest in clothes. I wore the dresses she made from leftover material without paying much attention to how they looked.

But my discovery of a new world of learning and my decision to enroll at the Seminary in the fall have sparked a new interest even in things as mundane as pretty clothes and hair.

At the apartment Max welcomes me with enthusiasm: "Let me look at you. You look splendid! You've grown again." Unlike other times, tonight he keeps eyeing me with a quizzical look. Suddenly he exclaims: "Now I know! It's the exuberance, a new vitality. It's very feminine," Max laughs with delight at his discovery. "I couldn't figure out what's different about you tonight. You've grown, to be sure, and so did your hair. The sun gives your hair that shocking blond tone. It's spectacular. And this colorful outfit does great things for you. And yet . . . it's the sparkle, a certain radiance, that's what makes the difference. It's devilishly feminine. Don't you agree?" Max turns to my brother, whose eyes glare with irritation.

"Cut it out, Max. You talk too much." My brother's annoyance at his friend astounds me. It is so unlike him—Bubi is not given to flares of temper. In a flash I understand: Bubi is protecting me from the male world. Bubi's concern is strangely reassuring. It makes me happier than I have been in years.

A Long Day

Bratislava, July 1, 1946

The streets of the city still slumber in an early morning haze as my rapid steps carry me toward the girls' seminary in Bratislava. From the corner of Svoradova Street I can see a group of children and adults milling about a faded yellow bus parked in front of number 7. Are these children my charges? My God, I am not ready to meet them yet.

When I reach the crowd, I make a bold attempt to escape into the building unde- tected. Just as I am about to pass through the front entrance, someone calls after me: "*Slečna?*" Miss?

Reluctantly I turn around and face a young woman with two little children in tow. "You are with the transport, aren't you, *Slečna?*"

"Hm, yes. I am."

"You see, *Slečna*, these children here are going with you. I can't wait for the transport to leave. I am late for work," she says with a note of urgency, pushing a little girl with light brown pigtails toward me. "This is Ruti . . . and this is Marko, her brother. Come on, Marko." The small boy, who has large brown eyes, refuses to budge. The woman gives each a light peck on the head. "Have a good time in camp." Once again she gently shoves the two frightened children toward me. "*Slečna?* Would you keep an eye on them until the transport departs?"

Without giving me a chance to explain that I am not the counselor and I know nothing about little children, the young woman is gone. Stunned, I stare after her as she boards a tram across the street. And I am left on the sidewalk with a heavy heart, a heavy canvas bag, and an even heavier responsibility for two little children I have never seen before.

Ruti, who looks about seven, pulls away from me and runs to join her little brother, who has climbed onto an enormous trunk on the sidewalk. The little boy, not more than five years old, his feet drawn up to his chest, shoots a defiant glance in my direction.

"Can you wait here?" I ask the two children.

"I have to go inside, but I'll be right out, okay?" Then, as an afterthought, I place my bag next to the children's trunk. "Can you do me a favor? Can you keep an eye on this for me until I get back?" They look at each other and nod in unison, and I sense a softening in their attitude.

Inside the building, a frantic hustle and bustle bespeaks a late start. Young men, women, and children dash in every direction, tripping over bundles of all sizes that clutter the corridor.

All at once I spot my counselor, Frieda Gelber, and hurry toward her with a sense of relief. She flashes a quick, preoccupied smile and brushes past me on her way toward a row of children lined up against the wall. She hands out a slip of paper to each child and is soon joined by another organizer who pins a yellow tag on each child's lapel. I stand there at a loss, not knowing what to do, when a voice calls out: "Ah, Elli Friedmannova. There you are. Have you been given your assignment yet?" It is Emil Block, the administrator. "Would you grab this clipboard and check each name on the list against the children lined up in the hallways and in front of the building? Please underline the missing names. And when you're through, bring the list to my office, would you please?"

"Oh, of course." I reach for the clipboard as if it were a lifeline. Remembering Ruti and Marko, I decide to start the roll call in front of the building. The two children's faces brighten when I approach and call their names. All the other children also respond readily when their names are called, and I feel a sense of relief. Thank God. These are normal, alert, and bright children.

I continue the roll call in the building, and here the children also respond with the same lively attention. A second list comprises the names of teenage boys. I find this group congregating in one of the rooms. At the head of the list, the name Sruli Goldstein is marked. Who is Sruli Goldstein? I have not heard that name mentioned before.

Just as I complete the roll call, a tall, young man with striking blue eyes enters the room. "Are you in charge here, *Slečna*?"

There is a touch of mockery in his tone. "Oh, no. I'm only checking the group against the list. I'm only an assistant counselor."

"Oh." The blue eyes radiate amusement, and I feel my face turn crimson. "My name is Sruli Goldstein," he says somewhat patronizingly. Suddenly I am tongue-tied. As I do not respond, he continues: "I'm in charge of the boys' group. We will be neighbors."

I still cannot think of an answer. Sruli Goldstein, with the most dazzling smile and blue eyes I have ever seen, again breaks the silence: "What is your name, *Slečna*?"

"My name? Elli . . . Elli Friedmannova," I stammer. Then, to make up for my awkwardness, I go on: "Leah is my Hebrew name. Leah Friedmannova. I like to be called by my Hebrew name."

Why have I talked so much? Why have I told him I liked to be called by my Hebrew name? I've made a fool of myself.

"Glad to meet you, Leah Friedmannova."

"Glad to meet you, too," I mumble, and then I run down the hall to Emil's office with the list of children's names, my face burning with embarrassment.

Soon children and luggage are loaded onto the bus, and I take charge of Ruti and Marko.

Now the two little children eagerly hold my hands. We have become friends.

At the train station I see Sruli Goldstein again as he and his husky young assistant direct the group of teenage boys into the train car. Why is Sruli Goldstein mocking me?

On the train a slender, middle-aged woman introduces herself. She is Mrs. Gold, our cook. She helps arrange the children's bundles on package racks and under seats. Remembering some of their names, I manage to organize the children's seating arrangements: little ones near toilets, older ones near windows.

The train carriage is stiflingly hot, and the children complain of thirst. Frieda begins filling cups with lemonade from a huge thermos, and I am handing them out, cup after cup after cup, into a sea of small hands. By the time I get to my seat we have been traveling for almost an hour, and I am overcome by fatigue.

I close my eyes and allow a myriad of impressions to filter freely through my mind. My apprehension is gone. The Sruli Goldstein episode has dissolved into oblivion. It has been a long day. So much has happened since I left Šamorín.

A small, sticky hand on my knee wakes me from my reverie. As I open my eyes, I stare into a pair of enormous dark eyes set in a pale, almost translucent complexion. The large face seems out of proportion to the three- or four-year-old body. It is the face of an adult.

"Tell me a story, *Slečna*." The tiny, plaintive voice is barely audible. "I'm scared."

I put my arms about the strange little figure and draw her into my lap. She seems weightless.

"What's your name?"

"I don't know. They call me Bronia."

"You don't know? Who calls you Bronia?"

She shrugs. "Tell me a story, please, *Slečna*. I'm scared."

Who is this child? I must ask Frieda about her. But first, a story for Bronia. What kind of story would suit her?

"How old are you, Bronia?"

She shrugs again. "I don't know."

I hope my shock does not show. What is the matter with this child? I clasp her closer to my bosom and embark on a story about a lost kitten. Bronia's face lights up with excitement as I let my imagination run wild and spin a tale centered around a brilliant and brave little cat. As the kitten's adventures grow more and more thrilling, they start to draw an ever-growing audience. All the other children draw near, taking up positions on every available place near me. Little boys and girls sit with eyes open and mouths agape in rapt attention. Ruti and Marko, who were sitting on either side of me, now snuggle up close, Ruti resting her head on my shoulder and Marko proprietorially pressing a chubby little hand into mine.

The tale takes on a life of its own. As my audience grows, I am compelled to raise my voice above the clatter of the speeding train so the children sitting at some distance do not miss any of the details. It is stifling hot in the car, the air is charged with electricity, and my voice is growing hoarse.

"*Slečna.*" A large hand rests on my shoulder. "You've been talking for over two hours. Talking for so long over the din of the train is exhausting. You're wearing yourself out." I raise my head in surprise, and our eyes meet.

This time the blue eyes are not mocking. They hold genuine concern. "Children, why don't you let *Slečna* take a little rest? She can tell you the end of the story a little later. There will be plenty of time for stories. The Tatras are still very far." Sruli Goldstein's smile is not patronizing as he advises me, "The children, too, can take a nap now."

I am grateful. "Thank you, Mr. Goldstein."

The children are disappointed, but do not protest. One by one they return to their seats. Sruli tips his hat and makes his way back to his group of teenage boys at the other end of the car. I lean back in my seat as both Ruti and Marko rest their heads in my lap, and within seconds, all three of us are fast asleep.

Frieda wakes me with a light tap on my shoulder: Would I help her hand out sandwiches and lemonade for lunch? By the time the children finish lunch, we have to get them ready to disembark at Poprad for a change of trains.

Poprad marks two-thirds of the journey from Bratislava to Vyšne Ružbachy. The radical change in the climate is astonishing. After descending from a hot, stuffy train carriage, we are buffeted by gusts of cold, crisp mountain air. All around us dark green hills rise in sudden, unexpected immediacy.

The children's teeth chatter from cold. Frieda and I quickly bundle them up in sweaters, jackets, raincoats, and scarves pulled out of their luggage, and herd them to the platform where the train for the High Tatras is to arrive. Here the station house provides some shelter. By the time our train pulls into the station, the sun is setting in a blaze of orange and red, and the distant hills turn purple.

The ride from Poprad to the High Tatras stretches the limits of my capacity for absorbing sheer natural beauty. The suddenness of vertical cliffs reaching to infinite heights not more than an arm's length from my train window assaults my senses with unexpected force. Waterfalls cascading from tips of hills are inches below the sky, and giant trees swaying in menacing altitude on razor-sharp, snowcapped ridges are unmistakable messages of immortality. Divine secrets tangibly, ungrudgingly communicated.

It is a puzzling message. How can such unstinting beauty share the planet with

Auschwitz? How can it coexist with the specter of the Holocaust?

Suddenly, I remember: This is the route our boxcar traveled to Auschwitz. Two years ago, these very tracks carried the train from our hometown eastward toward its destination in the death camp. Just like then, the train snaked ever upward on fabulous mountain passes.

I need answers. I need to understand. I need to understand.

It is late at night when we arrive at Vyšne Ružbachy. At the dark, deserted station a row of open carriages wait to take us into the hills. The horses battle a cold wind as they plow ever higher, ever closer to the brilliant starry sky. On the peak of what must be the tallest mountain, the carriages halt. We are on top of a dark, blustery world under a shimmering sky. The sheer expanse of star-studded sky above and the infinite depth of darkness below us are overwhelming. We have arrived at our destination.

The Certificate

The Tatras, July 7, 1946

Brilliant sunshine and the chirping of a thousand birds wake me. What time is it? I hop out of bed and run to the next room. The beds are empty. I run down the corridor and find every room empty. Where is everybody? On my first morning I have overslept!

Alarmed, I run downstairs and follow the sound of soft chanting. In the large hall, the girls are in the midst of morning prayers. One girl serves as leader, or pre-cantor, and the others chant the verses in response. I have never seen anything like it . . . adolescent girls conducting communal prayers in Hebrew.

Watching the scene, I feel like an outsider. Silently I withdraw and continue my search for the little children.

As I pass the dining room I see Mrs. Gold busily setting long tables for breakfast, in the company of my little charges, still in their pajamas.

"Good morning! How long have you all been down here?"

"Oh, the bright light woke us all early." Mrs. Gold smiles. "The little ones have been helping me set the tables."

I herd all six of them to their rooms to wash and dress, and then down again for breakfast in less than half an hour. At the breakfast table Frieda leads the children in reciting the blessings for the food, then explains the meaning of each blessing. I am familiar with the various blessings for food, one for bread, another for cakes and cookies, a different one for milk and other drinks, and one for fruit and vegetables. This morning, however, I learn that there is also a blessing, *brakhah* in Hebrew, to be recited when encountering natural phenomena like thunder and lightning, or when seeing the ocean for the first time.

How fascinating . . . this impromptu affirmation of a phenomenon when experiencing it. As a child, I remember the terrifying impact of a sudden thunderclap. By reciting the *brakhah*, "blessed be you, our God, king of the universe, whose power and might fill the universe," you sublimate your fear into a dialogue with God.

Here in these fabulous mountains I encounter a new spiritual dimension. I realize that Judaism is in essence an ongoing dialogue with God. As a matter of fact, all human experience is an ongoing dialogue with God.

I am infatuated with the mountains, the green forest, the radiant sky, and with knowledge. I learn to love Frieda, my intermediary to all the new things I am learning. There is a magic circle about her. During meals, during formal class periods, and on long walks in the hills, she dispenses knowledge—lessons in the Bible, Jewish ethics, history, and rituals. She also teaches us modern Israeli dances and songs.

My responsibility is to care for the two little boys and four little girls. During the older campers' formal class periods, I play catch and tell stories. During rest periods, I practically devour the books in Frieda's personal library.

After dinner the boys' camp joins us, and

the two counselors, Frieda and Sruli, conduct shared study sessions. At these times I am one of the pupils, listening and learning with unquenchable thirst.

The Sabbath crowns the week with a perfect combination of the worldly and the spiritual. In the morning Sruli leads the prayers and delivers a lecture in the open, under the unfathomable sky. The afternoon is taken up by discussion groups and singing. We hold hands and dance in a circle to lively tunes, or lock arms and sway to the melancholy melodies until the shadows grow long and it is time for dinner in the dining room.

Togetherness. Harmony of spirit. Beauty of nature. Learning. This day is closest to my idea of perfect bliss.

On Sunday morning, a lone bicyclist appears on the front path of the villa. As he comes nearer, I recognize him. It is the mailman from the town. Mail on Sunday? He waves a piece of paper in the air. It is a telegram addressed to Slečna Gelberova. Frieda opens the blue envelope with trembling fingers. One glance at the message, and Frieda's face is flushed. She closes her eyes as she clutches the paper to her chest and just stands there, motionless. "My certificate!" she cries. "It has come! Can you believe it? Can you believe it?"

The CERTIFICATE. The British immigration permit to Palestine. The passport to happiness. She is one of the lucky few to receive this coveted document. She applied over a year ago. Since then she has hoped and prayed, and then despaired of ever receiving it. And now, this morning, the miracle has happened. The certificate has reached her, here in the remote mountains.

All the children begin to sing and dance around Frieda. Happiness overflows into the hills beyond the villa, into the trees, the clouds.

We are due to return to Bratislava on August 25. "How wonderful," I say. "You'll reach the Land of Israel by Rosh Hashanah. And in the meantime, you'll have plenty of time to get ready for the great journey. Mentally. Even physically."

Frieda does not hear me. "I know there's an overnight train for Bratislava. It leaves here early in the morning. There are transports on Tuesday. I can make it for the Tuesday transport."

Tuesday? Which Tuesday? I must have heard wrong. I search Frieda's face. But her face is averted.

"I must pack immediately. It takes time to get down to the village to buy a ticket."

"Frieda, what do you mean, 'get down to the village to buy a ticket'? To leave when?"

"Tonight. I must leave tonight."

With mounting panic I shout, "But you can't! You can't leave just like that! What'll happen to the children? Who will lead them? Who will teach them? Who will take care of everything?"

It is only at this moment that she takes notice of my distress. "Don't worry, Elli. I'll send someone in my place. I'll see to it that another counselor is sent here immediately. By tomorrow evening another counselor will leave with the six P.M. train. She'll arrive Tuesday morning. You'll be okay for one day, won't you? Don't worry, you'll manage for one day. Elli, you'll manage better than you think."

Frieda turns and, with hurried footsteps, goes to her room to pack.

Frieda's news reverberates through the

little camp like an electric charge. The little ones cling to her, even the older girls cry unabashedly. Seeing the children's reaction adds panic to my anguish. Yet I have to cope with my angst and alarm without any outward sign.

After the horse-drawn carriage departs with Frieda, the abandoned camp resembles a wake. I am unable to console the children. I cannot make any promises. I know I cannot fill Frieda's shoes, not even as a second-rate substitute, even if I had resources of strength and knowledge. And I am fully aware that I have neither.

"Tuesday morning we are getting a substitute," is the only promise I can make. "She'll arrive bright and early on Tuesday. Until then, we will all have to be brave."

This promise is also my only consolation.

I Will Make It After All

I have asked Mrs. Gold to wake me at dawn. I can never wake up on my own, and rising at dawn is anathema. Yet I have to make an early start. I must participate in the morning prayers with the older campers, and then help the little ones wash and dress. My God, how will I accomplish all this?

The teens refuse to get up. "There is no point in getting out of bed," they argue. "There is nothing to do."

"We will work out a program," I promise with an artificially cheerful tone. "We will work it out together."

"Frieda is gone," they counter. "Nothing matters."

"Well," I suggest, "perhaps we can discover things that matter. I will listen to your suggestions. We will work out a program that will make everyone happy."

"We will never ever again be happy," they reassure me, "now that Frieda is gone. We do not care to be happy."

No matter what I propose, no matter how much I reason and cajole, it is all met with a stone wall of resistance. Finally I lose my temper.

"No more arguments!" I shout. "All of you, get out of bed. This very instant! Wash and dress, and get downstairs to prayers in twelve minutes! Not a second less."

I rush into the bathroom and lock the door. What have I done? Why do I always lose my cool? Involuntary tears begin to flow down my cheeks. I am supposed to be a grown-up, and I behaved like a baby.

What shall I do now? I will ignore the teens altogether. Let them do as they please. Let them fend for themselves. I will take care of the little ones only. But what happens if the little ones also refuse to cooperate?

I wash my face and wait a few minutes. I cannot appear in front of them with red eyes. Regaining my composure, I emerge from the bathroom and with dignified footsteps make my way to the little children's rooms. As I pass the two adjacent bedrooms of the teens, I see they are empty. The beds are made, and the bedclothes are neatly folded on the shelves. When I reach the downstairs hall, I find the girls sitting quietly, with prayer books in hand, waiting. They are waiting for me.

"Fine," I acknowledge in a firm tone. "Let's start. Who was the pre-cantor yesterday?"

"Rivka!" Alice is always the first to speak. "All last week Rivka was the leader. But Frieda said from now on we'll take turns."

"Did she appoint someone for today?"

"No, she didn't. May I be the leader today?" Alice's eagerness prompts her to hop up and down like a yo-yo.

"That's not fair," Minka, a sturdy, freckle-faced girl interjects. "I'm older than you. I should be the leader."

"I'm the oldest here. I'm fifteen and a half." Miri, a tall, skinny brunette raises her arm. "I should lead the prayers." I, too, am fifteen and a half. How fortunate none of the girls is aware of this.

"What's the difference? I'll be fifteen next month!" Minka volunteers, her voice rising.

I have to stop this bickering before it gets out of hand.

"Okay, let's draw up a chart according to birthdays. Whose birthday comes first?"

The idea works like a charm. Within seconds the girls are deeply involved in making up a birthday list, and the day is saved. The prayers get off to a lively start with Miri as pre-cantor for the day, and I hurry upstairs to help the little ones get ready for breakfast.

Marko is sitting in bed, crying. "I don't feel well. I don't want to get up."

Marko's face is flushed. I touch his head—it feels hot. What do you do when a child has fever? I remember that Mrs. Gold had children before the war. She would know what to do. I must run to the kitchen and ask Mrs. Gold to come examine Marko.

"Children, I'll be right back. In the meantime go to the bathroom and brush your teeth." Little Ruti also begins to cry: "I'm not supposed to leave my brother. I have to stay with him. I have to take care of him!"

I know it is useless to reason with Ruti. "Okay, stay with your brother. I'll be right back." As I am leaving the room, Elka, the youngest, starts sobbing.

"What's the matter, Elka? Why are you crying?"

By now I am desperate.

"I'm sick. I'm not feeling well."

"What hurts you?"

Elka shakes her tear-stained face. Nothing hurts her. She is just not feeling well. She cannot get up.

"Ruti, please take care of Elka, too. I'll be just a few minutes."

Mrs. Gold helpfully interrupts her chores in the kitchen and follows me upstairs to serve as medical consultant. She examines Marko by touching his forehead with her lips and feeling his neck with her fingertips. Her diagnosis: Marko has fever and swollen glands. Elka's checkup yields good news: She is not sick. No fever. No swollen glands. Yet she sobs uncontrollably as I dress her and she refuses to stand on her feet. I have no choice but to carry her in my arms to the dining room. Once I seat her next to the table, she resumes her loud wails.

The teens have finished breakfast. On the spur of the moment, I decide to hand out "work assignments" to them. The two oldest are sent on an "important mission" to the boys' camp to fetch Mr. Goldstein. One is appointed the task of taking breakfast upstairs to little Ruti. Others, of straightening up the little campers' rooms. A number of girls serve as my "assistants," helping me to feed the little ones at breakfast.

Elka continues crying and refuses to eat, despite all my assistants' coaxing. Finally, I draw her into my lap. Instantly she stops crying. Tentatively I bring a spoonful of cereal to her lips. She begins to eat with a hearty appetite. The problem seems solved. As long as she remains in my lap, Elka keeps eating cheerfully, eventually finishing her breakfast.

Before breakfast is over, Sruli appears in the dining room, with the familiar patronizing smile on his face. "Slečna Friedmannova. Problems? What can I do for you?" There is more than a touch of mockery in his tone.

"We need a doctor, Pan Goldstein. Or some medicine. One of the little boys is sick. He's upstairs in bed."

"May I see him?"

"Of course. This way to the bedrooms."

Sruli's facial expression turns serious after

visiting the feverish Marko. He offers to send two boys to the village for aspirin and to call a doctor if Marko gets worse. In the meantime, he volunteers to take the older girls to join his study group and to bring them back for lunch. I sigh with relief and gratitude. Thank God. I will manage the little ones, somehow, by myself.

After the older girls have gone with Sruli, I gather the little children in a circle on the carpet in the vicinity of Marko's room. I begin to tell a story, loud enough for Marko and Ruti to hear. Soon my little audience is deeply absorbed in the story, and Marko's rhythmic breathing reveals that he has fallen asleep. When the story is finished, I succeed in coaxing Ruti to join us, and we all go down to the garden to play.

The children are quickly caught up in the game. Their cheerful laughter dissipates my heavy burden. Suddenly I feel as if I could fly. Mrs. Gold agrees to watch Marko, and I take my little group on an expedition into the nearest wood.

When the children clamor for a story once again, I hit on the idea of teaching them a lesson in physics. "The Secret of the Rain Cloud," is the title of my story. How does rain happen? In the course of the tale, the children marvel at the discovery that water can evaporate and clouds are made of vapor that rose to the sky from lakes and rivers. They are fascinated with the notion that cold air causes clouds to compress and precipitate rain, and the cycle begins anew. They laugh out loud when I point out that the clouds hovering above were once rivers and lakes, and even the ocean. When the children beg for more, I continue with the story of snow, hail, and fog, and they plead that I repeat the tale over and over.

I do not notice that Sruli and the older campers have been trailing right behind us, listening intently to my tales. All at once, a rustling sound makes me turn. A loud cheer rings out, followed by a burst of applause.

"Bravo! Bravo!" They all shout with faces beaming. Sruli cheers loudest: "Go on! Go on! Please don't stop. We all want to hear. Very interesting lecture." Is he mocking me again?

"Please, go on. We want to hear more," the teens join in.

I continue, describing the water's composition of different elements, explaining what distilled water is and how it is made, pointing out the difference between rainwater and well water. And how a rainbow comes about.

By the time we reach the villa, it is time for lunch. I have to promise them all that I will continue my stories after lunch.

When we sit down to lunch I know my battle has been won. A sense of contentment permeates the atmosphere. The little ones cluster about me, vying with each other for a seat near me. The pain over Frieda's absence is somewhat slackened.

Perhaps I will make it after all. At least until Frieda's replacement arrives.

"Until Mommy and Daddy Return"

In these past three weeks I have come to know the older campers and their life stories. We have grown together, and I feel deep personal affection for each. This morning Rivka is the pre-cantor, and the prayers take on a special, animated quality. I believe it is Rivka's dynamic personality that resonates in the group. I love to watch them during morning services. As I watch them individually, I watch as many separate worlds. Separate tragedies.

Miri, a tall, slim girl with a long neck and slightly buck teeth, is a retiring day-dreamer. Her clear white skin, brown eyes, and fine features are accentuated by dark brown hair parted in the middle and tucked behind her ears. Miri has no relatives at all. Her parents and little brother were arrested by the Gestapo when their hiding place in a mountain cavern was discovered. At the time, Miri was away playing with children of friends hiding out in an adjacent cave. She is now living with this family "until her parents return." Nothing has been heard of them since their arrest three years ago. But the prospect of their return is a constant, unhesitating allusion. This is an element of post-Auschwitz mentality. Everyone about whom there is no specific news is expected to return. Over a year has passed since the end of the war. Many, many have not been heard from. Yet, they are expected to return. No news is good news.

Edita, a quiet, chubby eleven-year-old, has an older brother in the boys' camp. The two children, who are cared for by an aunt "until Mommy comes home," witnessed "Daddy choked to death in our garden by a group of rough men." They were members of the "Hlinka Guards," followers of Andrej Hlinka, the Slovak Nazi who looted Jewish homes and businesses and attacked Jews on sight. Edita's face seems to reflect both the memory of her father's violent death and the expectation of her mother's homecoming. Anguish and hope in equal measures are etched in her childlike, vulnerable features.

Herta, the slight, soft-spoken blonde with pale blue eyes and hair like cornsilk, never lets go of her brother's hand. She is only eight but acts as mother and protector to six-year-old Milo. Although the two children have found a home with a distant relative, Herta believes Milo's care and comfort is her sole responsibility. And the little boy responds in kind. He clings to his sister's hand as to a lifeline. Although he cannot read or follow the Hebrew prayers, Milo sits docilely holding hands with Herta while his peers are at play in the bedroom.

Herta and Milo are too young to remember their parents. Herta was only four and Milo two when the Hlinka gangs burst into their home during the night and dragged the parents out of their beds to an unknown fate. Neighbors found the frightened children in the morning and took them into hiding together with their own family. It was there that the two turned into extensions of one body, a Siamese-twins unit, and they continued that way even after the war, when the neighbors adopted them. "Until our Mommy and Daddy return."

Alice is twelve but looks older. She is tall for her age, and the light brown braids piled on top of her head make her look even taller. Her oval face is dominated by large hazel eyes that dart restlessly in every direction. Always in a state of perpetual motion, high-strung Alice is appealing and lovable in her bristling disquiet.

Alice is the only camper who has a parent. Her mother survived the camps but suffers from tuberculosis and has been hospitalized ever since her reunion with Alice thirteen months ago. Passionately devoted to her ailing mother, Alice talks of her visits to "Mommy" in the TB sanatorium incessantly, her face alight with longing and pride. She, too, was hidden in a "bunker" in the Carpathian Mountains while her parents, two sisters, and a brother were in Polish concentration camps from which only "Mommy" returned.

From the start the sisters, twelve-year-old Ester and ten-year-old Jutka, have sought out my company; they sit near me and walk alongside me whenever they can. The little striking brunettes are refugees from Hungary and have not yet learned to speak Slovak. I am their primary avenue of communication, as the other children know only a smattering of Hungarian. Both girls show early signs of great beauty. Lone survivors of a large family from Budapest, they were smuggled into Czechoslovakia en route to Eretz Israel by *Briha*, the illegal underground railroad Miki spoke about. They are sheltered in the Home until Youth Aliyah operatives arrive to smuggle them across the border to Vienna, and from there to the Italian coast. They have been waiting, together with many other children, for a Haganah boat to take them across the Mediterranean to a youth village in Eretz Israel.

Alzhbeta, sitting next to Jutka, does not seem to follow the prayers. I suspect that she has not mastered the Hebrew characters and is only pretending to go along. During the war she was hidden in a convent and received no Jewish education. An angelic child with a pink bow on her head and dark blond curls reaching her shoulders, Alzhbeta moves about gingerly, like an exquisite china doll, unaware of her surroundings. A rose-colored bubble seems to envelop this fairylike creature who never mentions her parents and does not expect them to return. They were shot by a firing squad on the bank of the Danube while Alzhbeta was picking berries in the woods nearby. The little girl was found by the nuns, and the convent became her home till war's end. Her father's brother found her after the war and adopted her. It was he who brought her to the Home and enrolled her in the Beth Jacob School so that she could learn about her Jewish heritage. But Alzhbeta has been unaffected by her Jewish education and environment in the Home, just as she was untouched by Christian teaching at the convent. Now she is sitting and staring out the window while humming a soft tune. What is she looking at? What is she thinking about?

Medi, a serious girl with an ascetic, narrow face and long auburn braids, is absorbed in religious devotion. The thirteen-year-old is well informed about most aspects of Jewish custom and ritual, and is zealous in performing them. Together with three brothers, Medi is a resident in the Home on Svoradova Street in Bratislava.

I see Bronia tiptoe down the stairs and slip quietly into her seat. She is the skinny little girl with the large head and enormous eyes who begged me for a story on the train and who puzzled me by knowing neither her name nor her age. Later I learned a little more about her background. When she first came to the Home, she could not speak. She gave no answers, asked no questions, did not cry, laugh, or complain. She was a silent little creature without a name, age, or history. She was part of a transport of children handed over to the *Briha* at a Polish border town. The *Briha* smuggled the children into Czechoslovakia and across the Carpathian Mountains all the way to Bratislava, looking out for the children's safety. They had no time to find out about their histories.

The young girls who cared for these children in the Home believed the tiny creature was deaf and dumb, or brain damaged. She recoiled from all human contact. When the girls attempted to remove her rags, bathe and dress her, she did not claw or kick or strike out, like many other children, she only huddled in a corner like a frightened animal, silent and withdrawn. Months went by and she did not respond to the name Bronia the girls gave her, or to the affection they lavished on her.

Until one morning. The girl on duty entered the children's room to help them dress, and to her astonishment Bronia greeted her by name. *"Dobré ráno, Gitta!"* Good morning, Gitta! "How are you this morning?" Bronia called cheerfully in perfect Slovak. Gitta almost fainted, but pretended to remain calm.

Soon it became apparent that Bronia's speech and mind were unimpaired. She knew her surroundings, the names of all the children and grown-ups in the Home. But her own name she did not know. Neither did she know her age or where she came from. She knew not a word of Polish, nor did she have any recollection of other people outside the Home. So she has remained Bronia, the quiet, withdrawn little girl who has been sometimes stubborn but never violent or hostile. Bronia has been the favorite in the Home, pampered by all yet unspoiled by all the pampering.

As Bronia sits down she makes a slight

scraping sound with the chair. Rivka glances in her direction, and the semblance of a smile crosses her intent face. A pretty girl with light brown hair, blue eyes, peachy complexion, and dimples when she smiles, Rivka is chanting the last paragraph of the prayer, and all the girls join in. Rivka commands her peers' attention with natural ease. And this competence extends into the realm of personal relationships, where her easy charm softens the sense of authority. If only her mother, her father, and her siblings were alive to see her now, so lovely, with so much promise.

I am suddenly overwhelmed with pain as Rivka concludes the prayers, and all the others chant amen. So many tragedies. So many young, promising, ravished souls. What does the future hold for them?

Preparing for the Climbing Expedition

The Tatras, August 4–10, 1946

It is the first full week of August, and no counselor has arrived as replacement for Frieda.

We have settled into a comfortable routine. The older campers happily carry on with
their practice of conducting prayers by themselves, and take turns preparing study sessions on subjects they learned at the Beth
Jacob School during the past term. I love
these sessions. They give me an opportunity
to learn, and give them an opportunity to
teach. I believe there is no better way to learn
than by teaching, and there is also no better
way to gain self-assurance. And what we
teenagers need more than anything is self-
assurance. We need it even more than love.
Our egos are continually starved for nourish-
ment. Will we ever be free, secure adults?

Since I cannot contribute to my campers'
knowledge of Judaism, I proposed to conduct

classes in subjects I learned during the past school year—physics, chemistry, math, health, geography, nature, and Russian. My proposal was greeted with enthusiasm. I set about devising games, quizzes, and competitions as framework so that even the little campers can participate in these sessions, mostly held in the shade of the pine forest encircling the villa. It has given me great pleasure to see the little ones just as attentive and as eager to learn as their older peers.

In two weeks our vacation will be over. All summer I watched the mysterious distant hills with yearning and have dreamed of climbing one of them. Finally my fervent wish has come true. Next Sunday we are going on a mountain-climbing expedition to the highest peak in the area!

It will be an all-day hike for the older campers, boys and girls. When I proposed it, Sruli thought a mountain-climbing expedition was a marvelous idea, and he helped me work out all the details.

Mrs. Gold has agreed to care for the little ones when the two camps, together with a professional guide familiar with all the trails, set out at the crack of dawn for the mountains. It was Sruli's idea to hire the friendly guide from the village, Shmuel, who offered his services within the first week of our arrival.

Yesterday I took the girls to the village to buy good climbing shoes, extra shoelaces, and fruit.

We are agog with excitement. All day Friday we prepare sandwiches and pack knapsacks.

Sabbath is a glorious day. In the morning we conduct joint prayer services with the boys' camp, in the open air. In the afternoon all the boys and girls sit in a large circle on the hillside overlooking the valley while Sruli delivers his weekly Sabbath discourse. The haze of July is gone; August glitters with diamondlike brilliance, revealing an endless row of peaks stretching to the horizon. Tomorrow we shall climb the highest among them!

Sruli and the boys leave for their camp at sunset. Long shadows swallow up their silhouettes, one by one, as they begin their downward path. Sruli's silhouette is last. Just before vanishing, he turns to wave. Or does he? I cannot be sure. The night is closing in rapidly.

It is bedtime. We must retire early and rise before dawn, to be ready for meeting Sruli, the guide, and the boys at the gate precisely at five A.M.

After putting all my campers to bed, Mrs. Gold and I check on the provisions. Food parcels, drinking vessels, first-aid kits—everything is in order, carefully packed in individual knapsacks.

Mrs. Gold gives me a warm hug. "Much luck tomorrow, young lady!" she calls heartily. "And don't worry about the little ones."

"Thank you, Mrs. Gold," I reply, and hug the kind, generous lady in return. "Good night."

As I lie in my bed, the crisp night air ruffles the satin curtains. Anticipation of the climb, the excitement of the challenge, the sense of responsibility—and the thought of spending the day in Sruli's company—fill me to the brim. And keep me awake for a long time.

Oh, God, am I entitled to such happiness?

A Rude Awakening

The Tatras, August 11, 1946

It must be past midnight when I finally fall
asleep.

Heavy pounding downstairs shakes me out
of a deep trance. What time is it? It is still
dark. Who keeps pounding on the front gate
at this hour?

In a daze I crawl out of bed. Now I hear
hurried footsteps, whispered voices.

"Don't open the light, Mrs. Gold. Hurry,
and call Miss Friedmann. I must speak to her
at once. Please hurry." It's Sruli's clipped
voice. Urgency reverberates in the dead of
night.

My God, what's going on? Groping in the
dark, I make my way toward the hallway,
where Mrs. Gold's slim, robe-clad figure suddenly appears.

"What time is it, Mrs. Gold? Why has
Sruli come?"

There's a quiver in Mrs. Gold's voice: "It's two-thirty A.M. I don't know, my child. Hurry downstairs. He wants to speak to you."

By the time I get downstairs, my eyes are adjusted to the dark, and I can see Sruli's tall silhouette against the front entrance.

"Miss Friedmann, listen carefully. We are in grave danger. The guide we hired for the climbing expedition came to our villa to alert me. Drunken partisans from the village are on their way here. We have to get out before they get here and harm the children. You have to get them out of here in the next ten, fifteen minutes."

"What do you mean, 'out of here'? Where to?"

"To the train station. We must leave here. To escape the partisans. They want to kill the children."

"You mean the climbing expedition is off?"

"Everything is off. Wake the children and get them ready. You must leave the villa by the rear exit. The boys and I can meet you in the clearing at the bottom of the hill in twenty, twenty-five minutes. The guide says there's a train for Bratislava at four A.M. That's our only hope of escape. If we hurry, we can make it. Can you do it?"

"I . . . I think so. How do we get to the train station?"

"On foot. I know a shortcut through the hills. Do you know the villa's rear exit?"

"Yes." On the day of our arrival I roamed the villa, my enchanted castle, and came upon the narrow, bolted door in the cellar. I unbolted it and followed the narrow trail as it wound its way to a clearing in the valley. From there the steeple of the church was visible and puffs of smoke from the passing locomotive reached me among the trees. That must be the shortcut to the train station.

"Miss Friedmann, hurry. Meet you in the clearing." Sruli shuts the front door soundlessly, and I dash up the stairs to the children's bedrooms. The next ten, fifteen minutes is all a blur. Mrs. Gold is already dressing some groggy little children, and I rapidly pull dresses, shirts, and sweaters over slumping heads. There is no time to explain. The older girls are bewildered as I goad them out of their warm beds and prod them to dress quickly, very quickly, in the dark. We are stuffing belongings in every available container—trunk, bag, basket, even laundry sack. Mrs. Gold dumps the sandwiches that were ready for the climbing expedition into pillowcases.

Without asking questions the unkempt children follow as we descend one flight of stairs. On the upper landing the grandfather clock shows five minutes to three. God, in five minutes we must be at the bottom of the hill! This is insane. In the moonlight the minute hand is like an eerie, elongated warning finger stretching to who knows where.

There is a sudden crashing sound. Huge pieces of glass hit the lowest stairs before we reach them. Another ear-shattering crash, and the grandfather clock tumbles and dissolves into a myriad of sparkling fragments seconds after the last child leaves the landing.

The little ones begin to shriek in fright. I take Marko on my arm and place my other hand over little Jutka's mouth. Mrs. Gold reaches out to calm the others. We virtually drag the children down the steep cellar stairs as more rocks crash through the villa's large windows. Luckily, the steady thunderclaps of the stone barrage drown out the children's hysterical shrieks.

They have reached the front gate and I can hear ear-shattering blows against the thick wood. Any moment now they will break through. God, save us.

We reach the entrance to the cellar. Marko's arms feel like a stranglehold about my neck as I bend down to force open the cellar door. Bronia is clinging to my right thigh. Several little hands are clutching at me from all sides. I am a cluster of clinging bodies as we make our steep, precarious descent. Mrs. Gold and the older girls are hauling the baggage on the spiraling cellar steps. Torchlights zigzag above as we reach the bottom of the stairs. They've broken through! They are in the hall, right above us!

"Mrs. Gold, shut the cellar door!" The cellar door creaks shut, and we are plunged into the depths of darkness, and deadly silence. As if by magic, the violent sounds cease, and even the children instantly fall quiet.

But we have no time to lose. Any minute the attackers will discover the cellar door. I must find the exit fast. I place Marko on the ground and with my free hand reach in the interminable darkness. Oh, God, help me.

Like in a recurring nightmare, strange yet familiar, I grope in the dark for an escape hatch. The wall is rough here, and a sharp metal object juts out. I bruise my wrist and feel it turn moist. Will our pursuers catch us by following the trail of my blood? God, let it be the door hinge! It's the hinge of the bolt. I grip it with all my might. God, help me! Help me!

The bar slides down with a creak, and the door swings slowly open.

Cold air rushes in through the open door. Moonlight falls on stunned faces. A collective gasp like a muffled shriek escapes from terrified lips. In panic, I whisper, "Children, please, not a sound."

We file out into the open, one by one. After the pitch-blackness of the cellar, the light of the pale moon strikes us like broad daylight.

Thank God, the trail is perfectly lit, and we begin our descent with relative ease. The children shiver violently in the bitter cold. The silence of the night is shattered only by the chattering of little teeth and the swishing of cold, wet foliage underfoot.

I pray under my breath as we advance steadily through the silent domain of the moon, the valley, and the forest. I pray that the children will keep walking, that we will reach the clearing in time. That we will reach Sruli and be safe. I pray that the next clump of dark shrubbery will not turn out to be an ambush, that from behind that thick grove ahead no rioters will suddenly pounce upon us.

There is no trace of the rioters here. The rioters belong to another planet. But who are they? And why are they after us?

Only later do I find out that they are former partisans drunk from their celebration of Partisan Week in the village tavern. Shouting obscenities against Jews, they left the tavern and went for their axes and pitchforks to "kill the little Zhids up there in the hills." In their drunken, murderous rage, the rioters meant business. Last year during the same week former partisans killed three Jews in Bratislava.

Finally we reach the bottom of the hill and emerge into a clearing. Thank God. This is the clearing for our meeting with Sruli and the boys. We've made it.

But where are they? Have we come too late?

What time is it? The clock tower is faintly visible. Oh, God, it's twenty minutes to four. We've missed them! They must have gone on to the train station. Mrs. Gold is whispering something, but I cannot hear. I cannot understand. We must follow Sruli and the boys to the train station. How far is it from here?

Hurry, Mrs. Gold. Hurry, children. We must make the four o'clock train. We must meet Sruli and the boys at the station.

The children's noisy breathing betrays their valiant effort at crashing on and on. Not a whimper escapes their lips as they march, shivering, on tiny feet through cold, wet underbrush. Twenty minutes to go. Let's move faster. Children, please, just a little faster.

The path is steeper here. The little children cannot make it. We must take them in our arms. The trail suddenly narrows into a wedge among the tall thicket. Breathing with effort, we force our way through hostile, heavy growth. My jacket sleeve catches on a branch. As I jerk myself free, I step up onto a paved platform. The train station!

Right before my eyes towers the gabled roof of the station house. Two rows of silvery tracks glisten in the moonlight. In the middle of the platform a white sign looms, and on it two words in black letters: VYŠNE RUŽBACHY. The clock tower is clearly visible from here. It's eight minutes to four. The train is due to arrive in eight minutes.

Children! Mrs. Gold! We have made it!

The station is deserted. Not a living soul anywhere. Where are Sruli and the boys?

"Let's go into the station house," suggests Mrs. Gold. "It must be warmer in there. And we can rest on the benches in the waiting room."

"The boys will never find us in the station house, Mrs. Gold. We must wait for them out here."

What if the rioters have discovered by now that we fled? What if they are following us and catch up with us here even before the train arrives? "Let's go behind the tall hedge. Let's wait there till the train comes. There we can rest on our luggage."

Like little rabbits we crawl through the narrow opening in the hedge and crouch on trunks and duffel bags. Bronia is sucking her thumb as she snuggles near me. Both Marko and Ruti crawl into my lap. Mrs. Gold and the older girls all take little children into their laps. From here we scan the platform, unobserved. There is no sign of the boys. Where are they? And where is the train? It must be four o'clock by now.

Have I made a mistake? Perhaps Sruli did not say four o'clock. Perhaps he said five o'clock. Or three? What if there was a train at three A.M. and the boys left with that train. What will become of us? My dear God, what shall we do?

All at once I hear a faint, distant rumbling. Does anyone else hear it? I'm afraid to ask.

"I hear something!" Rivka whispers, her eyes wide with excitement. "A faraway sound. Like a train."

"I hear it, too!" Alice crawls out from behind the hedge and stares in the direction of the sound. "I see it! It *is* the train!"

"I see it! I see it! It's coming. Children, the train is coming!" Several children are asleep. "Quick, wake up. The train is here!" We grab the children and the luggage and crash through the opening in the hedge onto the platform.

The train comes puffing into view, its headlights brashly piercing the faint glimmer of the dawn. Now it chugs to a slow halt, and in a flash the platform fills with a throng of passengers. Where did they all come from? The passengers virtually charge the train, and we join the onslaught. We carry the little children and force our way up the besieged rungs.

Here is a new obstacle to overcome. The train is frightfully crowded. It is a formidable challenge just to get past the entrance with unwieldy luggage and exhausted little children. We frantically shove and push. God, let us get past the entrance before the doors close!

I am on the verge of collapse. The whistle blows, the doors close, and the train is off.

We have made it! We are all safely in the train behind doors shut tight. The train is picking up speed, and the murderous mob is far behind. We have escaped and are going home.

Why Won't They Believe Me?

We face a ten-hour ride home pressed like sardines. We can barely move. Where are Sruli and the boys? They must be somewhere on the train. They must've boarded another wagon. In the last-minute, wild crush we missed them.

We must find a place somewhere for the little ones to sit. Shuffling around a bit, Mrs. Gold and I succeed in staking out a small sheltered area near a corner where we arrange the luggage to provide resting places for Marko, Elka, Ruti, Milo, and the other little ones. The older girls, Mrs. Gold, and I have standing room only. In time we, too, find ways to accommodate for the long journey. Some crouch on the floor, others drape themselves on armrests and on top of sleeping passengers. There are advantages to crowding. While the train rattles, shakes, and sways on curvy mountain passes, the tightly packed human mass keeps us propped up. I take hold of a pole, coil myself about it like a monkey on a tree trunk, and promptly fall asleep.

Oppressive heat greets us in Bratislava. A nebulous haze hangs about the bustling Slovak capital. The shrill street sounds and the stifling atmosphere filter into my awareness through a veil of fatigue. Vaguely I remember the question that has plagued me all along: What became of Sruli and his boys?

Like an army of zombies, the children, Mrs. Gold, and I trudge through traffic, dragging our bundles in search of some means of transportation. The smallest ones still cling to us, adding to the burden of baggage and exhaustion.

On a street corner we manage to hail a transport cab. There is room only for Mrs. Gold and the littlest ones, together with some of the baggage. The older girls and I make our way to the nearest tram station and climb onto a crowded streetcar heading in our direction.

At the Home our arrival causes surprise and consternation. What are you doing here? What has made you come back two weeks early?

Upon hearing our story Mr. Weise, Mr. Block, Malka, and Judith agree we made a wise decision in bringing the children home. They remember that last year there were riots here in Bratislava, too, during Partisan Week. "But that was last year, immediately following the war," Mr. Block reflects. "Another year has passed since then."

"Last year the country was still in the throes of war and violence, and things like riots still happened," Mr. Weise remarks. "People are more settled now. Violence is a thing of the past. It must have been some sort of noisy merrymaking, nothing more," he concludes. Then he adds in a sympathetic tone, "Still, it must have been frightening for you, whatever happened. You are still very young. Under the circumstances, your reaction is understandable."

My God. This is maddening. This is outright insane! Is there no one here who believes me? Where's Mrs. Gold? Where are the older girls? I'm too tired to respond. I'm too tired to think. All I want is to lie down somewhere and sleep.

People begin streaming into the Home to

pick up the children. There are exclamations of surprise, tears, hugging. At first the little ones refuse to part from me. My promises to visit soon prompt them into joining their caretakers and returning to their former homes.

Vaguely I continue worrying about Sruli and the boys. Emil, the director, reassures me: "Don't worry, Miss Friedmann. Sruli knows what he's doing. He probably decided to stay on, once things settled down. We'll probably hear from him soon."

"But that's impossible!" I practically shriek now. "Things couldn't just have 'settled down.' We were attacked by a rampaging mob. A mob bent on murder. They weren't going to 'settle down.' Sruli was there. He knew what was going on. He was the one who warned us to leave immediately."

"I understand. Believe me, Miss Friedmann, I do understand." Emil is trying to calm me. "Still, you have no reason to worry. Sruli knows how to handle the situation."

Now Mrs. Gold appears and explains how frightening, how dangerous the situation was. In my fatigue I hear only Emil's arguments. Is

Emil right? Did I act impulsively in running home? Was my panic induced in part by my vivid imagination? My paranoia?

No. No. No. I clearly remember: The escape was Sruli's idea. Where is he? Why didn't he join us, then? Why didn't he catch up with us at the train station?

I am very, very tired. I find an unoccupied bed in one of the bedrooms and lie down. Nothing really matters anymore. I am too tired to think. . . .

I hear someone calling my name. In a daze I make my way downstairs to find my brother waiting for me in the front hall. His face lights up in a broad smile, and he holds me in a tight embrace.

"You look great, little sister. What a deep tan!"

Instead of turning red and rising with blisters as in past summers, my skin tanned in the Tatras. For the first time in my life. "What's happened to your hair? I must say, it's striking blond!" Bubi eyes me with obvious approval. "And you gained some weight."

Sitting down in the dining room, I tell Bubi the story of the attack in the dead of the night and our narrow escape. "I'm very happy you came home," Bubi remarks. "I heard there were serious disturbances in the eastern part of the country, especially in the mountains. It seems the partisans rioted in many places and broke into Jewish homes."

Suddenly, I burst into tears. I cannot control my sobs. Repressed bitterness and a sense of relief have all surged up like a volcano. I needed someone to tell me I was right, that I had done the right thing. I keep wiping my tears away and smudging my face with hands still grimy from the long journey.

Bubi hands me his handkerchief. "Here, sis. Clean your face. Why don't you ever have a handkerchief?"

"I have no pockets," I snuffle. It is wonderful to blow my nose in my brother's large, clean handkerchief.

As we speak, there is a commotion in the entrance hall. A group of bedraggled boys are lugging heavy duffel bags through the hall toward the staircase.

The boys! Sruli's boys! They have arrived!

My drowsiness gone, I rush to the hallway. "Elli! Slečna Friedmannova. You're here.

Thank God." Sruli, deathly pale, his tall frame slumped with exhaustion, joins Bubi and me in the dining room. Emil and the others emerge from their offices to greet Sruli and listen to his incredible tale.

"Last night, on my way back to our camp after leaving you, I heard rowdy shouts rising from the eastern side of the mountain and realized they were approaching our villa. I ran and managed to get Shmuel and the boys out into the woods just before they got there. We hid in the woods while they ransacked the villa, calling for 'the cowardly Jews' to come out of their hiding places. With axes and pitchforks they smashed everything—the rampage was going on for over an hour. Then they burst out of the building and headed in the direction of your camp. . . .

"I hoped and prayed that you had left the villa by then." His voice now very hoarse, Sruli goes on. "I hoped you were on your way to the train station, a safe distance down the hill. We could not follow—they were blocking the path to the station."

When the inebriated partisans left, Sruli, Shmuel, and the boys went into their villa and hastily packed their belongings. "The interior of the villa was beyond recognition," Sruli relates. "The Slovak patriots turned it into a wreck."

"We reached the train station just as the four A.M. train pulled out. We had no choice but to hide in a dense forest on the nearby hill. There we waited until ten A.M. for the next train." Sruli gave a deep sigh. "In the meantime, luckily, the drunken pogromists must have returned to their homes to sleep off their strenuous adventures." And so when Sruli and his company of tired, cold, and hungry young Jewish boys boarded the train in broad daylight, no one was around to hurt them. Thank God.

My fatigue is gone. An unspeakable sense of jubilation fills my being.

"Thank the Almighty that you were no longer at the villa when they got there. They behaved like savages, ready for a massacre."

Sruli finishes his tale in a tired, hoarse voice. Like an old, old man he rises slowly from his chair and, without turning, walks out of the dining room. Emil and the others follow him. Are they going to thank Sruli for his superhuman rescue effort? Are they going to apologize for doubting me?

"I want to go home," I say to Bubi. "I'll go get my things."

"I'll cut my evening classes and go with you to Šamorín," Bubi declares. I want to leap into his arms and hold him tight. Instead, I only smile my thanks.

It is late evening when we reach Šamorín. Mommy is in shock. Her mouth agape, she stares for a moment, then shrieks, "Elli! What are you doing home?" She embraces me, then pushes me away to hold me at arm's length: "Look at you! I barely recognized you. You became a grown-up. A grown young woman!"

I am delirious. Such a compliment from Mommy is unheard of. But the most important verdict has not yet been pronounced.

"Have I gained weight?"

"I'm not sure. Perhaps. Yes, I do think you put on some weight. You look healthy. And tan! I have never seen you with a tan. How did you manage to get so dark? And your hair. What's happened to your hair? It is lighter than ever. Amazing how light your hair has become!"

This must be quite a disappointment. Mommy hates my being blond. She always wanted a daughter who was brunette. She always tried to darken my hair with a brew of chestnut hulks, but my hair remained stubbornly blond despite all of Mommy's efforts. Now the intense sun of the High Tatras has bleached my hair to an even lighter shade. Poor Mommy.

Mommy listens with horror to my tale of the partisan assault and our lucky escape.

"My God. Is Hitler not finished yet? Is the war not over?"

"We must leave this country as soon as possible," Bubi says during supper.

"We have not heard from the Foreign Office in Prague," Mommy replies. "It's been over three months now since we submitted our applications for a passport. And we haven't heard from the American Embassy."

"We must do something. We can't just sit idly by and wait indefinitely while things like this are going on. I'll ask around. I heard about other ways to get to America. Or Canada, maybe. There are always some new openings. We must not stay here."

Days Filled to the Brim

Bratislava, Winter 1946/1947

Next Monday an exciting new chapter in my life opens as a Seminary student in Bratislava. From now on I will live in the big city, in a dormitory among my peers, and visit Mommy in Šamorín only on an occasional weekend on a "free Sabbath," as it is called at the Seminary, when no specific program of activities is scheduled.

The girls' dormitory is a home for young girls from all over Czechoslovakia, Romania, Yugoslavia, and Hungary, some of whom were left without a single family member. The dormitory, comprised of two large rooms, a large shower hall, and five toilets, occupies the entire top floor. The large kitchen and dining hall are one floor down, and the study hall, auditorium, offices, and some of the workshops are on the main floor. In the basement are additional workshops where some girls learn trades and others work to earn some pocket money.

In the shower hall at least ten girls can shower simultaneously. There are only two showerheads, and sometimes, in a crunch, twelve or thirteen crowd under at the same time, competing for every bar of soap, even for every drop of water. We soap each other's back and shampoo each other's hair. It is marvelous to be part of such a large family. To have so many sisters. To share, share, and share. To be young, and to be together.

A new world of companionship opens before me, a world of intimate friendships, ideological debates, and learning. In the workshops, girls learn to make bed linens, men's shirts, silk ties, corsets, or dresses. Others learn leather work—making handbags, wallets, and belts. But the core of the dormitory is comprised of the Beth Jacob Teachers Seminary students.

I am one of sixteen young women who participate in the course. From eight in the morning to noon, and then from one to seven P.M., the sixteen of us share a long table where we listen to lectures and take copious notes on the Bible, Jewish history, the Hebrew language, general philosophy, and psychology.

It is an intensive course of study. In order to keep up with the pace, I must study late into the night, every night. I am the only student without any background in Hebrew or Jewish studies.

The Talmud teaches that there are four kinds of students: the sponge, the funnel, the sieve, and the strainer. The sponge is not selective; it absorbs everything, from essentials to useless trivia. The funnel does not retain anything: whatever it draws in at one end, it pours out at the other. The strainer lets the good wine escape but retains the slush! The sieve, on the other hand, lets the flour dust pass through and retains the fine flour. I am a sponge. I keep absorbing, without pausing to select. To me, every available bit of learning seems worthy of retention.

Feverish imbibing becomes my raison d'être. Once again I lose sight of important matters like clothes, makeup, and hair. My new, caring friends surround me with motherly interest and gently goad me: Why don't you do something with your hair? It's much too straight. Why don't you put a curl in it? Why don't you ever buy a new scarf? A pair of pumps instead of flats? A new belt? Why don't you use a touch of lipstick?

During my visits home, my mother pleads: "Elli, look into the mirror once in a while. Fuss with your appearance, just a little. Your eyebrows, for instance. They are so light, they are practically invisible. Can't you find out if there is anything, some dark dye, to color them?"

My brother has other complaints. "Why don't you stand still when I come to visit you? Must you always be so preoccupied?"

Bubi is attending the university now. He passed the gymnasium course for young people who missed out on learning because of the war. And then he passed the university entrance exams with flying colors. I am terribly proud of him.

He drops in to see me every day whenever there is a gap in his schedule. I am invariably in the midst of studying or doing chores. Although I am thrilled to see him, I am bristling with impatience to get back to my work.

For Mommy, my studies at the Seminary are of secondary importance. First and foremost she wants me to become a fine dressmaker, in preparation for America. Through some of Mommy's friendly contacts I have become apprenticed to Mrs. Magda Gellert, a dressmaker with a first-class professional reputation. Mrs. Gellert has graciously consented to accommodate my apprenticeship after my classes.

Although I like Mrs. Gellert, I am not happy at her workshop. I know manual skills are not my forte. Mother insists that sewing is not merely a manual skill: Fashion is the product of the mind, not just the hands, she maintains. She claims that thought and creative talent go into making a beautiful dress, that the lovely color and texture of the fabric enhance its style and elegance. But to me, fashion is nothing but meaningless frivolity, and dressmaking does not excite my sense of accomplishment. Mrs. Gellert, although an accomplished professional, is not an inspiring teacher. I find her sewing class sheer drudgery.

There is also the issue of my fellow apprentices' resentment. Because I had already learned the rudiments of dressmaking from my mother, Mrs. Gellert immediately skipped me to more advanced tasks and appointed me "senior apprentice." To add insult to injury, Mrs. Gellert insists on chatting to me in Hungarian during work, even though my fellow apprentices speak only Slovak, putting me in a painfully awkward position.

A tall, slim blonde with large, wide-set eyes, Magda Gellert could pass as a model. During long conversations while stitching, basting, and hemming, I find out that her maternal grandfather was a Hungarian count who converted to Judaism and became a disciple, then son-in-law of the Kalever rebbe, one of Hungary's leading Hasidic masters. The fabulous tale of her ancestry unfortunately culminated in the gas chambers of Auschwitz. After hearing her story, I understand the enigma of Magda Gellert's looks, the combination of very fair coloration, Gentile features, and deep dark eyes that hold indomitable sadness.

Twice a week I attend the Folk Academy for Languages to study English. At this academy, native speakers teach the languages through the audio-lingual method. My teacher, Mr. Bock, who lived in England for years, would tell a simple, often humorous anecdote in English and then ask us to repeat it verbatim. The power of repetition is astounding. It enables me to acquire proper diction, vocabulary, and grammatical skill. To my great delight, within a few weeks I am able to carry on conversations in English and to write simple poetry.

My days are filled to the brim. Between the teacher's seminary, the dressmaker shop, and the English class, I find myself rushing from one activity to the next.

No wonder my brother is annoyed with me for not being able to stand still even for a few minutes.

A Painful Parting

Bratislava, March 20, 1947

Three months have passed, and we have not received a response from the American Embassy in Prague about our position on the quota. In December news reaches us about a new U.S. emigration law under which young students and members of specific professions requisite for the United States economy would be granted "exceptional visas" to the United States.

Uncle Abish sends us a letter containing two student certificates. One for Bubi, from Yeshiva University, and one for me, from the Esther Schonfeld High School for Girls. These certificates, actually letters confirming our enrollment at the schools, qualify the two of us for "exceptional visas" to the United States. But what about Mommy? The list of "indispensable" professions does not include any that would qualify Mommy for a visa.

After a lengthy discussion, the three of us decide that Bubi should take advantage of the student quota and apply for the exceptional visa, and I should stay with Mommy and wait for our turn on the regular emigration quota. Once in America, Bubi would do his utmost to help expedite our case.

On March 6, Bubi's visa arrives. He is booked on a Swedish boat departing from Malmö on March 23. In order to reach Malmö by then, Bubi has to leave Bratislava by March 20 at the latest.

That's in two weeks! My God, why so soon? I ride a roller coaster of trepidation and thrill. Mommy plunges into stoic preparations. Bubi has serious doubts.

"How can I leave the two of you behind in Czechoslovakia? Apart from the anti-Semitic incidents last summer, political turmoil is brewing in Czechoslovakia," he says with a voice as heavy as lead. "And who knows what's going on with your place on the quota?"

Mommy reassures him. "Don't worry about us, Bubi. Just prepare for your journey with a peaceful heart. We'll be okay. Once there, you'll be able to help us. What can you do for us here?"

Bubi packs in slow motion. I cannot imagine my day without seeing his bright face at the bottom of the stairs. Without the radiance. Yes, that's it. Bubi is the light in my life. He's fun, ideas, humor, action. He is my source of information, insight, help, encouragement. I have a need to prove myself for his sake. I crave his approval, his validation.

I watch as he slowly, deliberately places his belongings into his luggage, each piece like a pledge of farewell. Every item is a part of me being locked in that suitcase. In the days that follow I fluctuate between resignation and deep despair. There are days when I go about the routine of living with composed determination. And there are days when I cannot bear the weight of his departure. I drag myself about on limbs of lead. I dread the moment of parting, but I preplay the scene over and over. Bubi's last embrace. Bubi vanishing behind the closing doors of the bus. The vehicle receding into the distance. The chasm between us filled with exhaust fumes.

March 20 is a Thursday. With a shudder, I

remember another March 20 not so long ago. Three years ago Bubi came home from Budapest unexpectedly, in the middle of the night, because he saw the invading German troops, he saw the Nazi swastika on their tanks as they rolled down Budapest's main avenue. An eternity ago he came home to warn us of the approaching doom. And now, on this day, Bubi is leaving home. Is it an omen?

Mommy comes in from Šamorín to see Bubi off. The three of us speak little on our way to the bus station. Is the oppressive silence due to their remembering this date? Or is it due to reliving past partings that governed life and death?

The bus stands near the designated platform, doors open. As passengers begin to file onto the bus, Bubi's face takes on a masklike hardness. He makes a gesture, as if ready to embark, and Mommy puts her hand on his shoulder. Her voice quivers slightly as she says, barely above a whisper, "Bubi, remember to remain a Jew, a good Jew. You must do this for Daddy. He would have asked you . . . "

A shock of embarrassment sweeps over me.

I cannot believe my ears. How can Mommy doubt even for a moment? "Mommy," I cry, "why are you saying a thing like this? How can you . . . ?"

But Bubi is silent. His eyes fill with tears as he throws his arms around me. "Take care, little sister." Slowly he walks up the steps onto the bus and hands his ticket to the conductor. Silently, I plead: Turn around, just once more, please. The conductor punches his ticket. Bubi turns around and flashes a brilliant smile, a last gift.

The doors close, and the bus begins to roll out of the station. Mommy says, "Let's go."

"No, Mommy. Not yet. Let's wait a little longer." For the same reason that I desperately want to wait until the bus disappears from view, Mother desperately wants not to. She is heading for the exit, and I have no choice but to follow her.

It is a chilly evening. Mommy and I dread returning home to Šamorín and facing the house, where every item is a reminder of my brother's absence. The Heino family, who are both distant relatives and close friends, have invited us to spend the weekend with them here in Bratislava. The invitation now seems like a godsend. So, instead of putting Mommy on the familiar faded green bus for our small town, I accompany her on a bright yellow streetcar to the Heino home on Edlova Street.

In the streetcar we hold hands, silently comforting each other. Tomorrow is Friday, and I have classes only until 10 A.M. I will spend the rest of the morning with Mommy, perhaps shopping downtown for small items unobtainable in our little rural town. To fill our gnawing inner vacuum with trivia. At the entrance of the building I say a quick good night. I must hurry and make it back to the dormitory before ten. As Mommy's solitary silhouette approaches the front stairs, I am filled with an ache. I run back to her for one more hug: "Good night, Mommy. I'll see you in the morning."

Mommy holds me a moment longer and presses her cold cheek against mine: "Good night, little girl."

I give a little chuckle at the familiar, loving epithet and run against the wind all the way uphill in order to reach the dormitory before lights out.

A Lost Child

Bratislava, March 21, 1947

I am too late. Lights go out at ten sharp, and now it's five after ten. Groping in the dark, I manage to fish my toothbrush and toothpaste out of the cupboard and make my way down the corridor to the bathroom, and then back again, to bed. As I slide under my blanket, I muffle a scream. There's a body in my bed! Mortified, I leap out. How could I have made such a foolish error and picked the wrong bed? Let me reorient myself. I peer at the face of the sleeping girl. Which of my neighbors is she? It is much too dark to make out her features. Let me find the empty bed. I tiptoe around several beds—each is occupied. Luckily, the streetlight illuminates the adjacent bed enough for me to make out the face on the pillow: It is Ellike Sofer, my best friend and my neighbor on the right. Then this *is* my bed! But who is the person sleeping in it?

What should I do now? There is no spare bed so I have no alternative but to share this one. Carefully I crawl back in and ease myself onto the narrow strip of space the intruder has left free.

Sleep eludes me. A notoriously restless sleeper, I toss and turn and lie in various positions during the night. Cramped by a bedmate, I cannot sleep. Who is this stranger who sleeps so soundly all night?

With the first glimmer of dawn I peer at the sleeping face but I do not recognize it. It is daylight when, overcome with fatigue, I fall asleep, only to awaken when someone's alarm goes off with a shrill clatter. It is seven A.M. My guest does not stir. Have I been sleeping with a corpse?

Groggily I get out of bed and make my way to the shower room. Somewhat refreshed by the cold shower, I begin to dress. The door of the metal cupboard creaks, and the corpse sits up in alarm. "Who are you?" she shouts indignantly.

"I was going to ask you the same question. How did you get into my bed?"

"Is it your bed?" she asks, somewhat mollified, and slips back under the covers. "I like it. It's a very good bed. And where did you sleep?"

"Where do you think? There are no empty beds. I slept with you. At least, I attempted to."

"You couldn't have! I didn't notice a thing."

"Of course not. You slept like a log. You took up all the room, and I teetered sleeplessly at the edge."

Now the large brown eyes stare in disbelief. "I'm a light sleeper. I would have noticed if someone got in bed with me. You couldn't have slept in this bed!"

I have no time to argue. "My name is Elli. Do you have a name?"

"My name is Rachel. I really liked your bed. Thank you."

"I'm happy to help out. Perhaps I'll see you later and find out how our little night romance came about. Now I must hurry to class."

But after class I have no time to return to the dormitory. I must hurry to Edlova to meet Mother for the shopping trip. In the evening Rachel is no longer there. Days later I find out that she, a former resident, had dropped in for a visit and decided to stay over. My neighbors had assured her I would be spending the night in Šamorín. The incident eventually forges a bond between Rachel and myself, a friendship that has endured for years.

By the time Mommy and I meet, however, my night adventure is forgotten, and the gnawing ache over Bubi's absence returns. But the anguish of this day is soon eclipsed by something that happens a few hours later.

The Heinos's charming four-year-old, Elka, talks us into taking her along on our shopping trip, together with her little playmate Jerry from next door. So we set out for the famous Manderla Building, the Slovak capital's eleven-story skyscraper, with two happy children on shiny red scooters.

The outing begins on a high note. Mother and I deftly squire the children and their scooters in bustling downtown traffic. They cheerfully follow us in and out of various shops, marveling at colorful displays.

By noon we purchase most of our necessities. "It's time to take the children home for lunch," Mommy reminds me, and I call to the children, whom I have just seen playing in front of a toy display. Elka scoots toward us and puts her little hand in mine.

"Where is Jerry?" I ask the little girl. Elka shakes her head, and her blond banana curls fly about. She does not know where Jerry is.

Little Jerry is not in the toy store. I race down the busy street, zigzagging among passersby, retracing our steps, all the time on the lookout for a little boy with a red scooter. I dash into every store we have visited. Have you seen a little blond boy with a red scooter? No one has. I rush around every corner we have turned; return to every shop window the children admired. He is nowhere. I race back to the spot where I left Mommy and Elka, hoping desperately to find him there. No luck. We question people on the street. No one remembers seeing a blond, blue-eyed, three-year-old little boy with a blue cap and a red scooter.

All afternoon we search for little Jerry, to no avail. Our anxiety turns to panic. What has happened to the child? He is from Budapest, a stranger in this city, speaking a strange language. How would he be understood? How would he find his way?

Has he been run over by a car? Has he been kidnapped?

Little Elka is hungry and tired, and inconsolable. Mother takes the sobbing little girl on her arm, and she soon cries herself to sleep on Mother's shoulder. She should be taken home for lunch and her afternoon nap. But I refuse to give up. "We must find Jerry. We cannot go home until we find him." Mother agrees, and we take turns carrying the sleeping child and her scooter as we frantically continue to comb the sidewalks and stores of downtown Bratislava. We ask policemen on their beat, the conductor of every streetcar that passes. Finally, a young policeman joins our search. He stops all pedestrians and instructs them to keep an eye open for a Hungarian-speaking three-year-old little boy.

It is getting late. Sabbath eve is rapidly approaching.

"Elka has to be taken home," Mother advises, her voice hoarse with tension. "I'll take her on the next streetcar, and you stay here to continue the search."

The young policeman finally advises me to report the missing child and have it announced on the radio. He directs me to the main police station on the riverbank. As dusk precipitates, I battle a bitter cold wind on my way toward the Danube, and by the time I reach the police station, I am near collapse. A stony-faced police sergeant takes the report and gruffly orders me to sign it. Then he issues a warning: "You, *Slečna*, bear full responsibility for the child," he announces sternly. "If the child is not found soon, or if he is found dead, you shall be arrested and put on trial for murder."

I burst into tears. The police officer is merciless: "It's too late for remorse now. Much too late."

I race out of the police building and across the wide-open square toward the radio station. Sobbing, I blurt out my message to the receptionist. He takes down the particulars of the case and passes the note to the broadcast room. The radio announcer emerges from his cubicle to reassure me that he is putting the item instantly on the air.

"Don't worry, young lady." The tall, thin, balding man has compassion in his voice. "The little boy will turn up. Someone hearing the announcement will surely come forward with information. You'll see."

"Oh, thank you," I say with a sob. "Thank you."

I walk out of the radio station into a dark, cold mist. It must be Sabbath by now; no longer can I ride on the streetcar. I take off for the dormitory at a run to change clothes for the holy day.

Nearing Svoradova 7 I can see candles flickering on the dining room table, and the girls assembled for prayer. I race past the open door of the dining room, past the kitchen, up the stairs to my room. I have no time to take a shower. I wash my hands and face in the bedroom sink, put on my Sabbath clothes, and quickly dash downstairs. In a flash I am on the street once again.

My heart pounds as I knock on the door of the Heinos's apartment. Mrs. Heino's face is glowing with delight as she opens the door: "Ah, Elli, it's you! Come in, come in. We have been waiting for you."

Sabbath candles are radiant in the silver candelabra. The salon is alive with people. Who are they? I recognize little Jerry's grandmother among them. She is smiling. Mother is beaming as she hurries toward me.

"Mommy, what's going on?"

Mother can barely control her excitement. "Don't you know yet? Little Jerry is here! He was home all afternoon. While we, panic-stricken, rushed about searching for him, he was home playing."

Soon I find out that the two children had had a quarrel, and little Jerry had lagged behind, sulking. A passerby, believing the child was lost, asked him where he lived, and when Jerry gave his grandmother's address as the well-known "Edlova" Building, the stranger took him to the building's lobby and left. When Jerry walked into the apartment, his grandmother assumed we all had returned from our shopping expedition.

As she was about to light the Sabbath candles, Jerry's grandmother was startled by the sound of her telephone ringing. Her telephone had been silent for years. Since the death of Jerry's mother, her only daughter, in Auschwitz, she had lived like a recluse. Bewildered, she answered the calls, all concerned inquiries and offers of help from neighbors who had heard the announcement over the radio. Then her doorbell began to ring, and neighbors began pouring in. Neighbors she had never seen before came to offer advice and solace. Once they discovered that little Jerry was safe and sound, they embraced the elderly lady with joy and relief. For the first time in years her home was filled with the warmth of human contact.

In her confusion, Jerry's grandmother rushed to the Heinos's house, all the neighbors following. Did Mrs. Heino know anything about the mysterious announcement on the radio? It was then that Mother arrived with little Elka in her arms, and they all understood the story of the missing child. Then Sabbath commenced, and Mrs. Heino ushered them all into her home.

They all welcome me like a heroine. Moshe Heino raises the heavy silver goblet brimming with red wine and recites the Sabbath blessing. The assembled guests chant, "Amen," and the goblet passes from hand to hand. I also take a sip of wine. All of a sudden, the room with all the smiling faces revolves about me.

When the guests leave, the grandmother's arms enclose me in a warm embrace. "Thank you, my dear, thank you. You'll never understand what you've done for me. What a great *mitzvah* you've done."

I feel dizzy. It is not only fatigue or the effect of the wine. It is happiness. My pain over my brother's leaving has turned into exultation. Instead of grieving over a departure, we are celebrating a return.

Dancing in the Square

Bratislava, November 29, 1947

At the end of May, classes at the teachers' seminary end, and we are in the midst of feverish study for the examinations.

The exams are a marathon affair, a true culmination of eight months of intensive, exhilarating study. For two days a panel of learned rabbis put oral questions to the sixteen of us in every subject on the course curriculum. We all pass with flying colors.

The graduation ceremony is a grand event. The entire Jewish community of Bratislava attends—communal leaders, rabbis, and relatives of the fortunate few graduates who have them. I am more fortunate than most. Tragically, none of the others has a parent present. The parents of Judith and Agi, who survived in the Budapest ghetto, are trapped behind the Iron Curtain in Hungary. The parents of all the others perished in the gas chambers of Auschwitz.

The day after graduation I am assigned to teach two classes in the Beth Jacob school on our premises and to conduct a study group on Saturday afternoons. At last I am a qualified teacher, officially certified and equipped with proper educational tools.

To top off the marvelous heady feeling, at the end of my first month of teaching I am offered a salary! Isn't life simply wonderful?

In the fall my teaching load is increased to four classes, and my salary is doubled. Now, instead of studying for classes, I prepare for teaching classes, late into the night, every night. My work with Mrs. Gellert and my study of English also continues apace. World events rush by, and in my many abstractions I barely notice.

One Saturday evening in November, after returning from the Heinos's in Edlova, I find the atmosphere in my dorm room charged with excitement. The girls huddle about Annie's shortwave radio.

"Girls, what's going on? What are you listening to?"

"Shush." Several heads turn. Pointer fingers are clamped on pursed lips like exclamation marks. "It's the vote."

"What vote?" My voice drowns into a hiss. "What vote?"

"Shush. The UNO vote. On Eretz Israel."

My God, I have completely forgotten. For weeks rumors have circulated that the big powers of the world would finally render a decision on Eretz Israel. At a meeting in New York they would vote to establish a Jewish State in Eretz Israel, turning our fervent dream into reality. And I, submerged in my million activities, had lost track at the critical moment.

Ears are plastered onto the set. I can't make out a word. All I hear is static. All of a sudden, there is a burst of noise, a distant implosion. What was that?

"I don't know," Annie whispers. The proud owner of the sophisticated set, Annie knows English and is our link to the Western World. "I'm not sure. The vote seems to be over."

"The vote is over! What are the results?"

We stare at each other. Annie turns the knobs. The static crackle grows louder. No one knows the results of the vote.

All at once the door bursts open, and Eva appears in the doorway, her face agog: "Girls, the big square before the Redute movie house is full. People are dancing around the fountain, right in the middle of the square . . . blocking traffic. It's wild! All the cars, buses, trucks are at a standstill. Hundreds are dancing. All the Mizrachi kids are there. I'm also going!"

So it has finally happened! I follow Eva up the stairs at a run to get my coat. "Eva, wait for me!" In a feverish haste many girls grab sweaters, coats, scarves. It's a nasty, wintry evening in late November. What day is it? The twenty-ninth. I race down the stairs, across the lobby, and down the front steps. Eva is nowhere.

I am breathless with the weight of the moment as I run up the street toward Michalovska Street, crashing into a flow of human traffic. Nothing matters. My sweat mingles with cold drops of rain. My hair is matted. My temples throb to the drumbeat of one thought: Eretz Israel . . . Eretz Israel, *naša svetá zem* . . . our sacred land, our home.

As I approach the Carlton Hotel, a powerful gust from the riverbank hurls the sound of singing toward me. A turn of the corner thrusts me face-to-face with a most incredible spectacle: The square is covered by a human carpet, a swinging, swirling, rhythmic carpet of thousands upon thousands—an enormous spinning wheel of dancers. The dancers are locked arm-in-arm, bopping up and down in the *hora,* the spirited dance of the Jewish pioneers in Palestine that has become a symbol of our movement. Triangular blue scarves with the Zionist emblem flutter in the wind.

I approach the racing circle and place my hands on the linked arms of two young girls as they whiz past. They instantly separate and welcome me into the circle, and we dance on, without breaking the cadence. I can feel the rush of cold, moist air as I dance faster and faster. It penetrates my throat as I sing, louder and louder. My hair flies in the wet wind, my feet slam against the wet asphalt, but my head is in the clouds. A thousand cars honk, and a thousand throats sing. The chime of the church clock filters through it all, one, two, three, four, five, six, seven, eight. It's eight o'clock. History is in the making. The Jewish

State is born. The theme reverberates in the breeze: "Eretz Israel, *naša svetá zem* . . ." Land of Israel, our sacred homeland . . . homeland. Homeland. Homeland. The dark, wet wind carries the message to the lusterless sky.

Eventually the magic circle slows to a halt, but it does not disperse. Not yet. Not yet. Faces glow with exhilaration as the singing starts up again, and arms remain locked. We want to hold on to the moment just a little longer.

Eretz Israel has just become a reality. Now the British can no longer keep the Jews out of the Jewish homeland. They can no longer prevent the refugee ships carrying young Jewish pioneers from landing on the shores of our land. No longer can they put Jews into prison camps just for yearning to step on the sacred soil of Zion, OUR LAND!

The gates of Eretz Israel will be wide open for us. The British "White Paper" is dead. No more restrictions. My God. My God! From now on we can go to Eretz Israel freely, whenever we want! All the refugees, from all countries. The Exile is over. *"And all the exiles shall return to Zion . . ."*

"*Shalom, havera.* See you in Tel Aviv!" A young fellow dancing near me unties his blue neck scarf and ties it around my neck: "See you soon, in Tel Aviv!" "In Haifa," his friend cheers. "In Haifa!" Others cheer and laugh. "In Jerusalem!" "In Beer Sheva!" "In the Galilee!" "At Lake Kinneret!" "On Mount Carmel!"

Savage, heady mood. Glorious, heady hilarity. Carefree, playful voices, hoarse from hours of singing in the wet, cold wind. Young boys and girls who have but recently returned from the realm of death are now drunk with the joy of rebirth. Young dreamers intoxicated with a sense of history are now experiencing its great moment. We are in the midst of a cosmic adventure like at Genesis . . . darkness is exploding into myriad fragments, like on the day God created heaven and earth. Hands reach out, to touch, to hold . . . to validate. Hands reach out to clasp other hands and shoulders, to caress cheeks, to unite in long embraces.

A last hug, a last clasp of hands, a last wave, and I am taking off at a run. I must hurry home, back to the dormitory. Back to a new beginning.

It is very late and very cold. I am all alone on my way home. Not one of the girls has caught up with me. What's happened to them? Something must have gone wrong. Our headmistress, Malkele, must have stopped them from going out. Why? Is it against the rules, dancing in public?

I can expect to face a stern rebuke. My stomach tightens, and I run faster as I contemplate the sobering thought. I brace myself for the consequences of what I have done. I am willing to pay the price.

A new epoch has dawned, and I was there to celebrate it.

Gina's Secret

Bratislava, November–December 1947

The lights are still on as I reach the dormitory. My roommates are preparing for bed. Malkele is nowhere to be seen, and I head for the shower room as unobtrusively as possible. Martha notices me and calls, "Elli, where have you been?"

"Shush. I'm going to the shower room. Talk to you later."

Martha follows me alongside the corridor. "People were looking for you."

"What people? Malkele?"

"No, Sori and Eva. They were anxious to know if you went to the square to watch the dancing. They, too, wanted to go, but Malkele stopped them and the others. She didn't let anyone go. No one knew where you'd disappeared to."

Thank God. I am safe. Martha Frohlinger is a loyal friend. To her I can divulge my secret.

"I did go to the square." I don't reveal what I did there. "It was . . . it was . . . you should have been there. All the girls should have been there!"

"We all wanted to. But Malkele did not let anyone go . . ."

"Martha, don't tell anyone I went, okay?"

"Okay, Elli. I won't breathe a word."

When I tiptoe into the bedroom, my friend Ellike Sofer sits up, agitated: "Elli, is it you? Thank God you're home! Where did you go? You said nothing about going out. Eva and Sori and the others saw you in the other bedroom, and then, suddenly, after the radio report, you disappeared. WHERE DID YOU GO?" Ellike's whisper turns into a hiss.

"I'll tell you later," I whisper. "After lights out."

Our beds are adjacent, and it is possible to whisper secrets without anyone else hearing them. I can trust Ellike implicitly, so I tell her everything about my adventure in the square. Although Ellike is happy for me, she is bitterly disappointed to have missed the momentous happening.

"You were dancing with the Mizrachi kids,

boys and girls?" She is incredulous. "Elli, were you holding hands with the boys? Who was there? Was Albert there?" Eva has a secret crush on Albert but never has an opportunity even to speak to him. We are not allowed to talk to the Mizrachi boys, or any boys at all, let alone dance with them! "Did you speak to any of the boys?"

"I did not speak to anyone in particular. We were caught up in the excitement of it all. We just sang at the top of our lungs and danced as if we were links in one unbroken chain."

We talk late into the night. For Ellike, tonight's event has deep implications. She has been waiting over two years for her turn on a transport to Palestine. Her cousin Moshe has been anxiously awaiting her arrival. As we talk, Ellike can barely contain her excitement. Who knows? She may be reunited with her cousin Moshe in Tel Aviv, perhaps in a matter of weeks! "Can you imagine? I may be in Eretz Israel for Hanukkah!"

We talk and cry for hours. Finally fatigue overtakes our excitement, and we grow silent. But I cannot fall asleep. Even after Ellike's rhythmic breathing tells me that she is sleeping,

I cannot drain my mind of tonight's deep impressions.

The next dawn brings news of disaster for the Jews of Palestine. The Arab states surrounding Palestine have called for a general strike, riots, looting. We learn the British have not changed their immigration policy. The precious entry permits continue to be limited. For months now, thousands of young Jews have been languishing restlessly in collection centers, expecting to go to Palestine. When will the Jewish State become a reality? Did we dance too soon?

One evening Gina whispers a request. Would I join her in her bed after lights out? She wants to discuss something important.

Gina's news turns out to be very exciting. She reveals that the Haganah, the secret Jewish army in Palestine, has headquarters and a training camp in Moravia. Many young Jews have been registering to join there. Gina's twenty-two-year-old cousin is being trained there, and when his training is finished he will be shipped to Palestine with Aliyah Bet, the illegal group circumventing the British embargo against Jewish immigrant ships. The young recruits are being trained for combat, Gina discloses, her voice so low, I'm not sure I'm hearing right. Girls are also trained for combat. But most are trained as nurses or field telephone operators.

"I don't intend to wait endlessly for the world powers to make decisions for me," Gina whispers. "I don't intend to wait while the Arabs are massacring my sisters and brothers in Eretz Israel. I've made preparations to join the Haganah, train for combat, and go to Eretz Israel with one of the illegal units."

Gina turns silent, waiting for my response. But I do not utter a sound. I cannot even breathe.

"They need us," Gina continues after a while. "My cousin Beni says there will be all-out war. Sometime next year the British are going to leave Palestine, and six Arab nations are poised to attack on several fronts. They need young people to defend the Jewish settlements. I'm going to undergo weapons training. I want to know how to fight." Gina's voice trails into virtual soundlessness. Chubby, soft-spoken, easygoing Gina. How can she say these things with such matter-of-factness?

How can she even think of holding a gun?

Gina's enthusiasm is contagious. With every passing day, my resistance to the idea of handling a weapon wears thinner. Finally Gina convinces me that hers is the only route to go. The answer to our people's survival lies in our fighting for the Jewish State. The UNO vote was only the beginning, a diplomatic formality. It is up to us to create a home for the Jews the world over, a safe haven from persecution. It is up to us to ensure a source and center of Jewish pride.

In a week Gina expects to be called to the training camp for processing. As soon as she reaches the camp she will speak to her cousin Beni about me. Beni has become a member of the staff, and Gina is certain he will make immediate arrangements so that I, too, can join soon.

No one at the Home must know about these plans, of course. The Haganah operations are secret, and the leadership at the Home would not approve of a girl joining a military outfit of any kind. I promise Gina to be extremely careful.

Briha

Bratislava, December 1947–March 1948

Miriam is shaking my shoulder: "Elli, wake up. I heard knocking at the main entrance. Please wake up."

Groggily I crawl out of bed. Miriam and I are sleeping downstairs in the children's dormitory. This week it is our turn to spend the nights with the group of small boys and girls recently brought to the Home from Hungary.

"Who do you think it is?" I ask with a yawn.

"I don't know." Miriam seems agitated. "Who on earth would come at one A.M.?"

I follow Miriam's tall, thin silhouette along the dark corridor. The entire building is wrapped in silence. No one, except Miriam, wiry and high-strung, has been awakened by the noise. We approach the front entrance. Carefully I place my ear on the door to pick up any sounds from the other side. All is quiet. Miriam must have had a nightmare. She has only recently arrived here with her mother, fleeing from Yugoslavia across a hazardous border. It's no wonder Miriam hears menacing noises in her sleep.

"It seems no one's knocking, Miri," I say soothingly. "Let's go back to sleep."

"But I'm sure I heard knocking," Miriam says apologetically as we cross the dark hallway and head for the nursery. "It was a light knocking. But it went on for a long time."

As we pass the pantry door, faint knocking is discernible from the back of the building.

"It's the back door," Miriam and I whisper in unison. As I approach the back entrance through the pantry, Miriam quickly slips behind the huge metal cupboard. She cannot take chances. She is an illegal alien in Czechoslovakia.

"Who is it?" I ask in an undertone.

"Slečna Friedmannova, is that you?" It's the voice of Emil, one of the administrators of the Home. His whisper betrays urgency. "Please open the door."

I quickly remove the bolt and unlock the door. Emil pushes the door in slightly, and through the narrow slit about ten people slip in, one by one, followed by Emil himself. Swiftly and soundlessly I lock the door and reinsert the bar. Emil leads the group through the pantry into the kitchen and quickly lowers the heavy window shades. Only then does he switch on the kitchen light. The sudden harsh light blinds me. Dazed with sleep, I gape at the unanticipated arrivals—a man, three young women, and six children. Clutching their meager belongings, their faces deathly pale and drawn with fear and fatigue, the little group forms an island of irrelevance in the middle of the kitchen.

"These people will sleep here in the children's dormitory tonight, *slečna*," Emil informs me. "There are extra folding beds in the pantry. Would you help me prepare them?"

Miriam emerges from her hiding place and helps us unfold the beds and make them up with blankets and pillows. After saying a few rapid words to the man, Emil turns to me again: "*Slečna*, I will be back here tomorrow morning. In the meantime, if the police or anyone else asks questions, you know nothing."

"How about Miss Seidel and Miss Gold-stein?" I ask, referring to our teachers.

"They know," Emil says with a nod. He pats the children on the back, tips his hat, and heads for the back entrance. "I'll see you all first thing in the morning." He quickly lets himself out the door, and I bolt and lock it for the night.

I attempt to say some words of welcome to the newcomers in Slovak, then Miriam does the same in Slovenian, her language. The newcomers do not respond at first. But when Miriam and I bring glasses of milk for the children, one of the women thanks us in Polish.

We show them where the toilets are and bid them all good night.

"They must've come straight from the Polish border," Miriam whispers when we retire to our beds. "They must've crossed over recently."

"They are refugees from Poland," Emil explains in the morning. "On their way to Eretz Israel. The girls were hidden in the woods, and the children are from a convent. Hopefully they will move on tonight. But it may take a few days. Please make sure they do not go near windows." Emil opens his wallet and hands me a hundred-crown note. "Please get them whatever they need. Ask the other girls in the dormitory to find storybooks and read to the children. They must be kept quiet by all means. These kids have been on the road for days."

The refugees from Poland stay for a week. All the girls are involved in making them feel welcome in our midst. By the time the escape route to Vienna is cleared and it is time for them to leave, we part as if we're family. We have all learned the hair-raising details of each life—the girls' narrow escape from the Germans and then their flight from the Russians; the children's lives in the shelter of a Polish convent; the young man's adventures in a Polish partisan unit. Their effusive gratitude for small favors and the children's hunger for affection have endeared them to us.

This encounter with Jewish refugees from Poland gives me new insight into happenings beyond our borders. For the first time I become aware of the conditions that confronted Polish Jews after their liberation from the Germans. I learn that hundreds were arrested by the Russians and put into labor camps, or sent to Siberian exile. Many of those who succeeded in escaping made their way to their former homes in small towns and villages, only to be met with hostile reception from their Polish neighbors. Pogroms swept some areas. Physically and emotionally devastated men, women, and children returning from prison camps and death marches had to flee for their lives once again. Their tales remind me of my excruciating experience in the Tatras last summer, and I feel obligated to help.

The contact with the four adults and six children from Poland is my direct initiation into the secrets of *Briha*. I had learned from Miki in Šamorín that *Briha* means "the flight" in Hebrew and that the *Briha* organization has established an underground network of escape routes from Eastern Europe to the West, and from there to Palestine. Because East European countries have sealed borders, and leaving without permission is a capital crime, these rescue operations are a dangerous undertaking.

Czechoslovakia is centrally located between East and West, and so most routes go through it, primarily through our city. Bratislava serves as a border crossing point to Austria, a way station to freedom. After crossing the Czechoslovak-Austrian border, and then an arduous land strip occupied by hostile Soviet troops, the refugees can reach the American Zone in Vienna—and freedom.

Thanks to its geographic location, and to the corruptibility of Slovak officials, Bratislava has become a virtual bottleneck of illegal traffic from the USSR, Poland, Romania, Yugoslavia, and Hungary. For exorbitant bribes, officials from border police to local commissars agree to look the other way on designated days when refugees from neighboring countries enter Czechoslovakia on the east and exit on the west. The loading and unloading of camouflaged trucks or freight trains and all other movement must be accomplished under cover of darkness, at the risk of the organizers and their charges.

The hazardous journey notwithstanding, they keep coming, the young and not-so-young, carrying the burden of their tragedies.

Their faces are turned toward the Middle East, where the Jewish State is floundering under the Arab assault. Some relish the challenge of fighting for the Jewish homeland. Most shrink from the thought of yet more war. But they keep coming, a constant stream of refugees.

I am assigned to serve as liaison. The *Briha* organization deems my "typically Slavic" appearance—straight blond hair and high cheekbones—ideal for the task. How ironic. Dr. Mengele, the Auschwitz monster, believed my appearance was "typically Aryan." While he sent thousands of children to their deaths, he ordered me out of the line that led to the gas chambers, and because of that I am here today to do a job that requires "Slavic" looks.

My task is to meet the transports at the outlying track of Wilson Station, now renamed Stalin Station, in the dead of night, and accompany them to one of the underground refugee centers, called "stores." The former Jewish elementary school, now an abandoned building, serves as one such "store." Furnished with army cots and blankets, it accommodates up to a hundred people.

A number of Bratislavian Jewish families have offered to put up refugees in their homes when the other centers are full. I bring new arrivals to these homes sometimes at one or two A.M. By using the secret code—a set of two long raps followed by three short raps on the windowpane or door—I alert the hosts to the clandestine arrivals, and they open their doors without delay. Through a narrow slit my charges slip in swiftly, and when the door shuts behind them, I make my way back to the dormitory as fast and as unobtrusively as I can. I hurry to catch some sleep before dawn, when other groups have to be escorted to gathering points in other parts of the city.

Sometimes there is a break in the process, the transport is delayed, and the refugees have to be sheltered for weeks. Then I make the rounds of all the hiding places every morning and respond to a multitude of requests: buy cigarettes, toilet articles, medication, make phone contacts, deliver messages. During these lulls I am busy nearly every hour of the day.

Despite the rare occasions when tension takes its toll and the refugees become fractious and quarrelsome, the *Briha* experience reinforces my confidence in humanity. The refugees display remarkable courage, discipline, and cooperation, a sense of humor and generosity of spirit. And my *Briha* colleagues display inconceivable self-sacrifice and dedication.

During my nocturnal expeditions I get to know people at their finest. The same people who during the day seem like ordinary human beings motivated by nothing nobler than the pursuit of material possessions, at night assume extraordinary stature. Like knights in shining armor they work with superhuman dedication during the long night, but the morning betrays neither their activities nor their larger-than-life human dimensions.

The Haganah Camp

Moravia, February—March 1948

Shock waves reverberate throughout Czechoslovakia. The Communists take over the government in a military coup. Our president, Edouard Benes, has disappeared. Our foreign minister, Jan Masaryk, son of Czechoslovakia's legendary first president, was thrown to his death from his bedroom window. The country is in turmoil. Daily, Democratic Party leaders, highly placed civil servants, and wealthy businessmen are fleeing to the West, across borders soon to be sealed by our new masters.

Crowds flood the offices of the American Embassy in Prague, clamoring for visas to the United States. But the American Ambassador has been recalled to the USA. For the next two days, the receptionists and clerks at the offices of the American Embassy, harried as they are, diligently jot down names and passport numbers on bits of paper. On the third morning, the stately gates of the American Embassy remain bolted; the beseeching multitude is deprived even of the illusion of hope the haphazard bits of paper had held. We are abandoned in the tightening grip of Communist claws—we are trapped behind the Iron Curtain.

A week later I board the train for the station in Moravia, the name of which Gina had divulged in secret. I have not consulted Mommy. I did not even mention the subject of Haganah during my visit to Šamorín last weekend. Once again I am caught on the horns of the old dilemma—America or Palestine; the family pact, or the Haganah. The clear-and-present expediency has won.

The Communist takeover is my cue. Mommy and I must find a way to get out of Czechoslovakia before the borders are sealed permanently. With America's doors shut in our faces, the Haganah is our only avenue of escape.

Gina has been accepted for combat training. Before leaving the Home last week, ostensibly to join relatives in Bohemia, she disclosed that Beni had arranged an interview for me at the Haganah training grounds.

The long train ride provides ample time for reflection, but I refuse to reflect. I know I've made a rash decision. But I also know we have no alternative. By the time I reach my station, I feel as if the last shreds of doubt have miraculously evaporated.

It is still early morning. Sparse snowflakes flutter in the crisp air as I descend from the train and look about with apprehension. How will I recognize the contact person who is to drive me to the camp? Just as I reach the platform, lugging my canvas bag stuffed with immediate necessities, a trim young man comes near, reaches for my bag, and whispers under his breath, "My name is Beni. Follow me."

Without responding, I follow Beni out of the train station. The two of us walk silently for about fifty meters, then Beni addresses me once again in a barely audible undertone: "There's a bus behind the station house. Don't look around. Just board the bus."

There are about fifteen young people on the bus, boys and girls. I take my seat in the third row next to a girl who looks a few years older than me. I nod with a smile, but my companion does not acknowledge my presence. I follow suit and do not introduce myself. No one speaks. A tallish young man joins the bus and with an imperceptible nod takes the driver's seat. Soon Beni enters and begins to battle the door of the bus in an effort to close it. At long last he succeeds, and takes the seat next to the driver. With a forward lurch the shabby conveyance takes off.

About seven or eight minutes later, when we are on the open road, the bus pulls over and the two men drape all the windows with khaki army blankets.

"Please do not attempt to move the curtains and look out," Beni warns quietly. "The location of the camp is a secret, known only to a few of us. I expect you all to cooperate. This entire operation is highly classified. Even the word 'Haganah' is classified. After your visit you are asked never to refer to it."

The drive takes about an hour. No one attempts to strike up a conversation. I sit with eyes closed and listen to the tree branches brushing against the bus with every bump of the road. We must be crashing through thick growth in heavily wooded terrain.

When the bus comes to a halt, Beni directs us to line up single file behind him. We follow Beni obediently through a dense forest until we reach a cluster of wooden huts camouflaged by tree branches. Do these few huts constitute the headquarters of the Haganah in Czechoslovakia?

As we forge ahead, treading on stiff, frozen undergrowth, I notice thick metal cords running from one tree to the next across a clearing. Quite unexpectedly, my bus companion whispers, "That's for paratrooper training. They train you to jump from those wires."

I am taken aback. Apart from Beni's curt instructions, this is the first human voice I've heard since morning. What's compelled her to speak to me now? How does she know about the wires? Is she permitted to disclose this? I don't reveal I've heard her remark, and we revert to our initial silence.

Beni points to a flat hut. "You can wait in there for your turn. And this," he says, pointing to the tallest of the wooden huts, "is where your interview takes place."

We are summoned one by one. Each recruit spends about half an hour in the command hut. When my turn comes, I find I'm a bit nervous. What if I don't look tough enough for combat? What if my answers are less than satisfactory? What if my rationale for joining is not acceptable? What if my mother's consent is required?

The young man with horn-rimmed glasses looks friendly, and I am somewhat relieved. He does not seem so tough himself. I believe he will find me acceptably tough. And, after all, who would guess I have a mother?

The questions seem simple. What's your name? Your address? Your father's name? Your mother's name? Your place of birth? Your date of birth?

"What? You're only seventeen?" The friendly face freezes: "Who sent you here? Didn't you know about the minimum age requirement?"

As if stung, he springs to his feet and races out of the room. A few minutes later he reappears with a taller, older-looking man, also with horn-rimmed glasses. The older man fixes me with a severe gaze. "Who sent you here?"

"No one sent me. I found out about this place from a friend. She's in training here." Instantly I regret the last sentence. Perhaps I am not supposed to be aware of training, or even use the word? My heart beats rapidly, and I feel the blood rush to my face.

"How old is she, your friend?"

"Twenty-one."

"Didn't she tell you about the age limit? We don't accept even eighteen-year-olds. I'm told you're seventeen. What do you expect to do here?"

"I . . . I don't know," I stammer. "To be trained. For Pal-Palestine. I want to go to Palestine . . . and fight, if . . . if . . ." I do not go on. Is the word "fight" classified? I shouldn't have spoken so much.

"We do not accept younger than eighteen and a half for training. This is not a game. Everyone who comes here jeopardizes our security. You should not have put us in this position." His voice is as hard as steel. "You will be driven back to the station and put on the next train. Return to your home and do not breathe a word to anyone about your little expedition! Understand?"

I feel like crying. He's right. My brother is right. I am a baby. Why do I always mess up everything?

The tall fellow's horn-rimmed face mellows. He rises and extends his hand. "*Shalom.* Come to see us in a year and a half. I'm afraid we'll still need you then. *Lehitraot.* Till then."

The jeep, camouflaged with tree branches, its windows draped with green army blankets, delivers me to the train station in less than an hour. The driver hands me my train ticket and points to a train on the nearest platform. "There. Your train is waiting. *Shalom!*" He salutes with a hint of a smile and disappears in a shower of dust and pebbles.

Once again, my dilemma is solved by powers other than myself. My sense of humiliation and guilt slowly dissipates as the train draws closer to Bratislava. By the time I mount the stairs to my dorm room, I am overcome by relief.

It is only three P.M. and I have lived a lifetime since early dawn.

"It Has Come to Our Attention..."

Bratislava, March 1948

As if an invisible hand turned off some light-bulbs in the sky, the entire spectrum of life has dulled immeasurably since the Communist takeover. All private businesses and industry are nationalized. All grocery stores, now called "Source," are homogenous little units with uniform exteriors and uniform items for sale. Textile stores, shoe stores, drug stores—each has lost its individual character. With the disappearance of competition, the initiative for improvement, courtesy, and even attractive packaging and window display has vanished. All forms of advertisement have become a thing of the past. Color is gone.

Movies and plays are censored. Russian films have replaced the American, French, and Italian films that had been the rage of Bratislava. The Russian films are propaganda vehicles designed to indoctrinate, not entertain. On the front wall of the Redute, the favorite hangout, drab black-and-white streamers proclaiming party slogans have replaced the colorful posters that had announced forthcoming events and attractions. Movie houses are empty. Coffeehouses and sidewalk cafes formerly brimming with life are now deserted. Fun has vanished.

No one complains. As a matter of fact, no one says anything. Silence has become a way of life.

And life goes on.

No one, except Gina, knows of my humiliating attempt to join the Haganah. Two days later I am summoned to the main office by a panic-stricken Martha. "They want to see you at once," she hisses breathlessly. "They are all there. Even Mr. Weiss. Malkele is there, and Judith, Emil, Leslie, and a man I don't even know. Even Rabbi Gruenberg is there. What have you done this time, Elli? This time it is very serious. Hurry. Hurry."

I am in shock. How have they found out? Gina would not, in a million years, squeal. Besides, she's not here. Someone from the

Haganah leadership? But why would anyone from Haganah disclose the affair? It makes no sense.

I walk slowly downstairs, preparing answers. I know I have to admit the truth. There is no point in trying to deny it. My only defense is the truth: that I could see no reason why any Zionist institution would object to Haganah. And the Home is a Zionist institution. The Haganah is fighting for the Jewish State. And there is nothing written in the Torah against fighting for the Jewish State. On the contrary: It's a *mitzvah*, a commandment. Why hadn't I told anyone about my plans? The Haganah operations are classified. Haganah discipline demanded that I do not reveal them even to my own mother. . . .

The committee members fill every available seat in the small office. The mood is solemn, but I do not detect any hostility. And yet, the faces are grave, and the atmosphere borders on funereal gloom. I can barely breathe.

"Slečna Friedmannova." MISS FRIEDMANN. Sounds ominous. Mr. Weiss, the president of the Bratislava Jewish Congregation, is speaking. "It has come to our attention"—here it comes—"that you have been serving as teacher in four classes of the Beth Jacob School. You have conducted classes in grades A, B, C, and D. Is that correct, Miss Friedmann?"

"Yes, it's correct." Both his daughters are attending my classes. Dinah is in grade B, and Rivkah is in grade D. Have they complained about something? They are lively girls but good pupils. I can't recall any confrontation that would have occasioned complaints.

"As you know, Miss Bock is leaving us," Mr. Weiss continues. "She is leaving us at the end of the week. Her position as headmistress is hereby vacant." Erica Bock, a tall, striking brunette, is getting married. Her engagement has been the talk of the dormitory. But what does it have to do with my Haganah fiasco?

Mr. Weiss looks intently into my face: "The committee has decided to offer the position to you, Miss Friedmann."

There must be something wrong with my hearing. The room begins to rotate slowly.

"Do you think you will be able to assume the responsibility, Miss Friedmann? Of course, one of the graduates will be assigned to assist you in teaching some classes, just as you have assisted Miss Bock. Naturally, you will receive the same salary as Miss Bock."

I'm going to be sick. The room is rotating much too fast.

"Miss Friedmann?"

"Yes?"

"The committee would appreciate the favor of an immediate reply."

My relationship to Miss Bock, a self-assured young woman with a prestigious diploma from the prewar Beth Jacob Seminary, has been akin to idol worship. And now I—how can I presume to take her position?

The members of the committee look at me questioningly. The faces of my two teachers, Malkele and Judith, are glowing with approval. My God, how do I deserve all this?

"Mr. Weiss, I wish to point out that I look much older because of my height. But, in fact, I am only a year older than the pupils in grade B. Does the committee believe me capable of assuming the responsibility?"

"How old are you, Miss Friedmann?"

"Seventeen."

Mr. Weiss looks around, canvassing the other members in the room: "What do you think, ladies and gentlemen? Miss Seidel and Miss Goldstein, what do you think?"

My teachers glance at each other for reaction. Malkele undertakes to respond and delivers a verdict that would top all the tributes that I have received ever since.

"Elli Friedmannova is mature enough for the position. That is why we have recommended her."

Mr. Weiss clears his throat: "So, Miss Friedmann, do you want the job? We would appreciate an answer."

I take a deep breath. "Oh, of course. I want the job."

They all stand up and, with a slight bow of heads, wish me *hatzlacha,* success. Even long-bearded Rabbi Gruenberg bows his head and murmurs *hatzloche.* I dare not smile. Standing on shaky legs I, too, bow my head and whisper: *"Dakujem. Dakujem pekne."* Thanks. Thank you very much.

The three of us, Malkele, Judith, and I, remain standing as the rabbis and community leaders file out of the office. After the men depart, Judith and Malkele put their arms about me, and I fight back my tears.

As I climb the stairs to my dormitory room, a flood of impressions washes over me. It was only two days ago that I was not deemed mature enough to be trusted with a gun. And today I am deemed mature enough to be trusted with children's minds. At seventeen I am not old enough to handle weapons, but I am old enough to mold children's souls.

Which requires greater responsibility: wielding a book, or a gun? Which is a more effective device, or a more lethal weapon: a gun, or education?

Vilo

Bratislava, May 15–September 22, 1948

It is a glorious spring after all. Eretz Israel
is free! Yesterday the British left the shores
of our land, and David Ben-Gurion, head of
the provisional government, read the Declaration of Independence to jubilant crowds in
Tel Aviv. After a two-thousand-year gap,
the Jewish nation once again has a home.
The ancient yet new Jewish State has an
ancient yet new name. It is called the State
of Israel.

"The State of Israel," I keep repeating to
myself, and with each repetition it sounds
more familiar.

A few days later news reaches us of a
massive Arab attack, from all sides, against
the newborn Jewish State. There is an all-out
war against the State of Israel, just as Beni
predicted. War, again. The young volunteers
trained by Haganah are needed urgently. Just

as the older Haganah man intimated in his parting words to me.

Gina is there now, in Palestine-Israel. Has she been assigned to combat duty? Has she perhaps already been engaged in combat? We hear high numbers of casualties, a high number of wounded. My God, is she among the casualties? We have no way of finding out. There is no direct communication with the State of Israel. The official news agencies report heavy fighting on all sides and predict a quick end to the Jewish State. Logic dictates their forecasts. Look at the odds, the radio commentators declare firmly. Massive Arab armies against a handful of undertrained, poorly equipped Jewish fighters.

But we dismiss the logic of the official line. We are bolstered by whispered rumors of secret arms shipments from Czechoslovakia to the Jewish fighters in Palestine, of clandestine donations of Czech airplanes.

We pray, and hope against hope. We remind ourselves of other battles, when Jews fought against overwhelming odds and won. We talk of the Maccabees. Weren't they, as history records, "few in number who overcame the many, the weak who overcame the mighty"? Didn't a handful of Jewish guerrillas rout the powerful Greek forces and liberate ancient Israel? And our ancestors in Egypt, didn't they, a group of oppressed Hebrew slaves, overcome the mighty empire of the Pharaohs and march out, a free people, "with heads raised high and with backs erect"? How about Joshua at the walls of Jericho? Didn't the fortified walls of Jericho crumble before a handful of Israelites? Miracles happened in the past. Miracles can happen again.

Several weeks ago Annie disappeared. A short time before her sudden, mysterious departure Annie confided to me that she was going to join a Marxist-Zionist youth organization somewhere in Bohemia. She hoped to get to Palestine with this group and work with them to build a *kibbutz* there. A *kibbutz* is a collective farm where boys and girls work and live together. I was puzzled by her secretiveness and her reverence for Marxist ideology. Only when, in great secrecy, Annie recited poems by a Slovak-Marxist poet, her idol, did her conduct become clear. The poems were quite radical, and their message was certainly far removed from the ideology of our Home.

I find myself thinking of Annie very frequently, especially since the outbreak of hostilities in Israel. Has her group reached Palestine? Have they formed the nucleus of a *kibbutz*?

Ellike Sofer is worried about her cousin Moshe. Finally, toward the end of the summer, some letters arrive. Moshe is in a combat unit. One of his letters encloses his picture with a group of fighters in camouflaged headgear. My God, the fighters seem so young, so vulnerable.

Daily, young men and women leave for Israel via Austria, Italy, and the Mediterranean Sea. Daily, Bratislava becomes emptier. Daily there are mass farewells at the train terminal. Entire families flee from Communism for countries willing to grant visas. Argentina, Venezuela, the Dominican Republic, and Australia are the most popular destinations. Most of my pupils are gone. My Beth Jacob school has dwindled to two classes.

Then, unexpectedly, I am offered a job in

the public school as a "teacher of Hebrew religion." According to a new law, every pupil is entitled to thirty minutes of instruction per week in the religion of his choice. Has my job been arranged by the *Briha* as a "front"? It entitles me to a governmental salary and membership in the Socialist Teachers Union. I am happy with the salary, no matter how small.

All government employees are required to donate a day's work per month for the benefit of the Party. The Socialist Teachers Union demonstrates the teachers' loyalty to the Party by lumping together the twelve days and donating them as one unit at the beginning of the school year.

During the twelve days we are to do "voluntary duty" assigned by the Party. On the designated morning in mid-September I arrive at the premises of the Union at six-thirty A.M. About seventy well-dressed men and women of all ages are gathered in front of the building, in a mood of obvious apathy. When our assignment is announced—we are to work on a road construction detail between Bratislava and Devin—a cloud of gloom envelops the entire gathering. Teachers on road construction?!

With sullen silence we are loaded on trucks together with hoes, shovels, and wheelbarrows, and are shipped to the construction site north of Bratislava.

As soon as we reach the open country high above the Danube, the mood brightens. The shimmering silver-blue river below and the breathtaking cliffs all about make our spirits soar. When one of the teachers calls out, "Let's dig in, ladies and gentlemen, the road awaits us," laughter reverberates throughout the ranks, and instant solidarity is born. In a spirit of high adventure we begin the work, and the sense of well-being does not desert us for the rest of the day. By the time we board the trucks for the journey home, we are elated at the prospect of seeing each other again tomorrow morning. We relish the thought of digging and shoveling and raking in each other's company from seven in the morning till five in the afternoon. Even the strict surveillance of die-hard Party "stool pigeons" does not diminish our anticipation of fun.

My partner, a sturdy woman of about

thirty-five, insists that I call her by her first name, Terri. At first we keep inadvertently banging our shovels together, apologizing profusely at each such mishap. Then we make a pact: no apologies. And this is the beginning of a friendly camaraderie between us. At each crash and clang we laugh uproariously, let wisecracks fly, and keep shoveling. Our rowdiness sets the tone for the others, and they all join in the banter.

The head foreman at the work site is a young man named Vilo. Rumor has it that his appointment to this exalted position has less to do with his expertise at road building than with his Communist credentials. Vilo is a no-nonsense Party official whose presence seems to intimidate even the other foremen. His towering figure dominates the work site. The dark blue uniform seems to accentuate not only his massive shoulders and slim waist, but his forbidding attitude. His small, piercing black eyes, framed by dark hair tucked under a dark blue military cap, seem to probe our soul. They scrutinize our dedication to the Party, the sincerity of our service.

When Vilo approaches, we instantly stop

all horseplay. We even stop talking to each other for fear of a word being misunderstood by Vilo. He does not seem vicious or ill-tempered, only zealous. Zealots are dangerous. Vilo's reputation of unquestioning Communist zeal and loyalty to the Party sets off warning bells whenever he approaches.

Vilo stops his motorcycle whenever he reaches our segment of the road. He surveys our work with a keen eye, asks curt questions, and issues curt instructions. Certainly, our raucous cheer has attracted his unwanted attention. I suggest to Terri and the others in our segment that one of us should serve as a lookout for Vilo. The lookout's warnings will give us enough time to wipe the last traces of amusement from our faces. It is obvious to all that Vilo is paying excessive attention to our segment. His much-too-frequent visits are making us all rather uncomfortable.

Moreover, Vilo almost always singles *me* out for scrutiny. I am the acknowledged troublemaker. Here, with an open vista of awesome beauty, and in the company of congenial colleagues, I have become as lighthearted and carefree as a child. I have turned into an impetuous adolescent, trading silly observations with my fellow "laborers," mimicking, teasing, and giggling without restraint. Vilo's attentions are a signal for caution.

All at once, Terri stops work and waves her shovel in the air.

"Hey, comrades! I've just realized something. I've had a brilliant insight! A revelation!" She shrieks with laughter. "I know why Vilo keeps stopping here and harassing Elli! Because he has a crush on her!" Shrieking laughter greets Terri's outrageous idea, and a barrage of quips follow: Vilo is searching for religion! He wants to convert to Judaism and needs the right contact, a teacher of Hebrew religion! Needs mothering! Ha-ha-ha! Elli, the maternal type; Vilo, a lost little boy! Elli, next time he stops by, just take him into your lap! More raucous laughter. Hilarity rises to an unprecedented pitch.

The next time Vilo passes our row I find it difficult to keep a straight face. I almost faint with fright when he turns to me and asks pointedly, "*Slečna*, why are you smiling?"

"I'm not. I'm not smiling."

"Yes, you are."

"I . . . I am happy. I like this work."

"You like this work? Like this better than teaching?"

"Well . . . of course this work is just for a short time. I don't know if I'd like it as much for my permanent job."

"I'm told you are a teacher of religion. The Hebrew religion. Is that correct?"

"Yes."

"Where did you study?"

"At the teachers' seminary on Svoradova . . . I mean Nešporova. Next door to the Catholic Theological Institute. We are Nešporova seven. The Theological Seminary is nine. Actually the building is the Theological Institute's dormitory. I think the Academy is elsewhere. At least that's what I've heard. I'm not sure." What's wrong with me? Why am I talking so much?

"I know the building. And you live there? Is your dormitory in the same building?"

"Yes."

"Where do you teach?"

"Palisadna. It's near the Nemocnica." The hospital. I deliberately omit the word Židovska—the full name of the hospital is

Židovská Nemocnica, Jewish Hospital. Am I trying to hide my Jewish identity? Why? After all, he knows I must be Jewish if I'm a "teacher of Hebrew religion."

Without a response, Vilo jumps on his motorcycle and is gone.

"Good. Very good." Jiri Slezak is the first of my group to speak. He raises his rake, sending a whiff of wet sand into the air. "We are getting somewhere. When is he taking his first lesson in the Bible?"

Laughter rings on all sides. I return the salute with my hoe and flick bits of wet earth into my face: "Soon. During lunch break. By five o'clock I will make him into a full-fledged Jew." Loud cheers and applause greet my announcement.

It is a rainy day, and we have been working in intermittent drizzle. To my surprise, at the start of the lunch break Vilo reappears. Collective eyebrows are raised.

"*Slečna*, where do you sit during lunch? Would you want to sit on that log under those trees? It's much drier there."

"All right." I follow him without a backward glance at my group. I can feel their looks, their suppressed chuckles. I cannot take the chance of locking eyes with them and bursting out in laughter.

I try to take casual steps as we climb up the mountain. Awkwardness controls my every move. I wait for Vilo to sit down on the log, then I take my seat at a respectable distance from his long knees jutting high into the air.

I fiddle with my sandwich bag, waiting for Vilo to talk first. Why did he ask me to join him for lunch? I wait for Vilo to start eating first. However, he only stares ahead, his elbows resting on his knees, his jaw resting in enormous upturned palms.

"What's your name?" he asks finally.

"Elli Friedmannova. And yours?"

"My name is Villiam Grentze. *Slečna*, may I call you Elli?"

"Of course. That's my name."

"I am glad we meet again, Elli Fried-mannova."

"Again? Have we met before?"

"I saw you some time ago. It must have been over a year ago, or even more, I'm not sure. But I'm sure it was you. The Zionists were dancing in front of the Redute, in Carlton Square. I saw you dancing among them?"

"Yes, I was there that night. It was the day the UNO voted on the Palestine Resolution."

"Are you a Zionist?"

"Why do you ask?"

"I want to know. Are you?"

"Well, I want the Jews to have a state of their own. I was very happy that it happened. Does that make me a Zionist?"

"Do you want to go to Palestine?"

"Yes, I do."

"That makes you a Zionist."

I am seized by momentary panic. For a member of the Socialist Teachers Union, this may be a dangerous admission to make. I quickly add, "But I am a loyal member of my union. I do not see any contradiction. One can be a Socialist and a Zionist simultaneously. There are Socialist communes in Israel. The *kibbutzim*. They are based on Socialist principles. Some are even Marxist. Did you know that?"

"Yes, I've heard. Do you also want to join such a commune? What is it called?"

"*Kibbutz*. Perhaps. I don't know yet. I want to continue my studies. I don't know if one can continue to attend school in a *kibbutz*."

I want to know everything about Villiam Grentze—his profession, where he lives. But I dare not ask.

The whistle signals the end of lunch break. Vilo slaps his knees with visible annoyance. "Damn it. And you did not even eat your sandwich."

"Neither did you."

"I don't have any."

"Do you want to share mine?"

Vilo nods, and I draw out two pieces of dark bread stuck together with jam and make a clumsy attempt to break them into two halves. The result is not very elegant. Vilo observes my predicament with an absent-minded smile, then takes one messy half and starts munching.

"Dakujem." Thank you. We walk silently down the wet slope. When we reach the bottom of the hill, Vilo mutters something under his breath, hops on his motorcycle, and takes off. I put my half of the sandwich back into the bag and join the others.

The group behaves delicately. No remarks. No questions. Not even amused looks.

"What's going on here?" I ask in surprise. "Don't you want to know?"

"It's entirely up to you." Terri speaks up with admirable restraint. "Do you want to tell?"

"Of course, I want to tell. Everything. Except, there's nothing to tell. Nothing. *Nie nada.* He asked my name, what I did, and where I studied. Then I asked his name."

"What is his name?"

"Grentze. It sounds like a German name."

"It's German, all right," Jiri Slezak pipes up. "Our hero has a skeleton in his closet. What else did he tell you?"

"Nothing of consequence. You want to know the real truth, the true source of his attraction? My sandwich. He's irresistibly attracted to plum jam."

They all speculate about when Vilo will be back. Milo Hussar suggests taking bets. Terri sets the stakes: "Let's count to thirty-five. I say he'll be back before the count of thirty-five. Who wants to top my bet?" Lenka Nemec bets on forty; Janko Vilensky on forty-six. All the others call various numbers, and I grow very self-conscious about the whole thing.

Will he show up at all this afternoon? And when he does, will I be able to act naturally?

The count begins, and Vilo appears at twenty-two. I am at once embarrassed and pleased. Vilo no longer makes pretensions of acting in a supervisory capacity or issuing instructions to any of the others. He stops his motorcycle right next to me and announces unceremoniously, "Tomorrow I will bring a sandwich for you. What kind do you like?"

"I . . . please, don't. I eat only kosher. That's a special diet. Please, don't bother. I can bring two sandwiches tomorrow. Is plum jam okay?"

"Plum jam is very good. *Dakujem, slečna.*" Vilo touches his cap with his fingertips in a brief salute and rides off, as briskly and unceremoniously as he has come.

Vilo does not return all afternoon, and the bettors are puzzled. I wonder: Have I hurt his feelings by rejecting his offer of a sandwich?

On the homebound journey the discussion focuses on Vilo. Seventy academicians are puzzling over a Communist Party official who does not quite fit the mold. Who is he? What makes him tick? How will he act tomorrow?

I am deeply stirred by Vilo's disclosure

that he met me on that memorable evening, the night of fierce passions, the night the State of Israel was born. I am torn by doubt: Is he a member of the secret police? Or, is he a Zionist sympathizer?

Did the Vilo episode actually happen, or did I make it up?

Before going to bed I prepare two plum jam sandwiches. If Vilo does not show, I can always eat a second sandwich.

This morning, shortly after we begin leveling a small elevation in an isolated area of the work site, Vilo unexpectedly appears next to Terri and me. He playfully snatches the shovel from Terri's hands and issues a mocking challenge: "Why don't you take a little rest and let me do your quota for a while?"

Terri happily takes up the challenge. She climbs on the hillside to her favorite perch, where she has a spectacular view of the Danube. Vilo, on the other hand, launches into a vigorous shoveling activity. We work silently side by side for several minutes. Then Vilo begins to talk about himself.

To the accompaniment of his rhythmic

shoveling, Vilo divulges painful, personal details about his life with stunning urgency. He talks about the dual trauma of his mother's death in Auschwitz and his father's self-torment over her tragic fate. Although he refused to comply when all the Germans were ordered to divorce their Jewish wives, he blames himself for his failure to save her life.

"My father is a good man. And he loved my mother very much. I pity him but cannot help him. I cannot even talk to him," Vilo concludes with a sigh.

"You *must* talk to him."

"I cannot. I cannot help him." Vilo works furiously. Then he asks, "How about you? I want to know everything about you."

I tell Vilo about my incarceration in Auschwitz and other camps, about my father's death in Bergen-Belsen, about my mother and brother, and my dilemma about Israel.

With a strange earnestness, Vilo says that he understands my feelings about Israel. I can sense his empathy, yet I am reluctant to ask questions. I want to know how he got involved with Communism, and what accounts for his high position in the Party. After some hesitation, I do ask one question.

"Vilo, on Carlton Square on November twenty-ninth, were you a spectator, or one of the dancers?"

At this moment trucks arrive with gravel and sand. Vilo takes a quick leave. He must hurry and supervise the unloading. Perhaps he did not hear my question over the din of the trucks' arrival. Or perhaps he has another reason for not answering my question.

During the next few days I find Vilo's company exciting and baffling all at once. As we get to know each other, I lose my awkwardness in his proximity. His friendship infuses me with a new self-awareness. I can sense dynamic strength and faith radiating from an inner source in Vilo.

I have never met anyone like him. Are my feelings for him inspired by compassion, or by gratitude for his having invited me to share his pain? Do I admire him for his powerful public image, or for the strength he displays in coping on so many levels? Do I find him so fascinating because of an unexplained element in his makeup?

In a short time Vilo has become a personal friend, and yet he remains an enigma.

The road construction project of the Socialist Teachers Union comes to a close, but Vilo has worked out a plan for us to see each other.

"I will come to Nešporova seven with my motorcycle and pick you up after our work, every evening," he suggests brightly. "I have a table at the Café Carlton. There we can continue our friendship."

"It is not possible, Vilo. I'm strictly Orthodox. I cannot keep company with boys. Especially with boys who are not religious."

"What if I become religious?" he asks in jest. "I can learn. I may even like it, especially if you taught me."

Meeting Vilo is out of the question. I would not openly flaunt the rules of the Home, nor would I cheat and see him surreptitiously.

"There is no way out, Vilo. We must accept the inevitable. This is the last time we will see each other. I am grateful to God for having met you."

Vilo vows he will find a way. He must see me, he declares firmly. "I have waited for over a year to see you again. God sent you to me. It

must have been ordained that we get together. It must be His will."

No amount of explanation changes his
determination to see me. I ask him to respect
my wishes and not come to the dormitory—
nor near the building. I ask him not to do
anything that would place me in an embarrassing position.

Apart from my restrictions about dating,
there is also the hazard of Vilo discovering my
work for *Briha*. For me this reason is even
more compelling.

At long last I succeed. Vilo promises to
stay away, and I know I can trust him. We
part with a firm, warm handshake.

With my teacher colleagues there are emotional embraces. Terri is inconsolable. "I
know I will never see you again," she sobs.
She proves right. Although we vow to visit
often, our lives away from the Bratislava-
Devin highway are worlds apart, and the distance is unbridgeable. So it is with the others.
Jiri Slezak, Milo Hussar, Janko Vilensky, and
Lenka Nemec. We all pledge to keep in contact, but we know it will never happen.

Our Last Chance

Bratislava, October 1948—January 1949

The enchanting September days in the hills above the Danube are followed by strenuous work with the *Briha* during a particularly brutal winter. The transports from Poland are a thin but constant flow throughout a November plagued by heavy snowfall and bitter cold winds. We are called upon almost every night, sometimes for a small group of people, other times for only a single individual. These lone arrivals have to be quartered for longer periods until a sizable transport accumulates.

The Slovak authorities are growing less and less cooperative. Stalin's high hopes for the establishment of a Socialist regime in Israel, which would guarantee him a foothold in the Middle East, are dashed. In Israel a Democratic government has come into being, and the Red dictator does not conceal his displeasure.

Stalin's open hostility brings about a dramatic shift in the attitude of the entire Communist bloc, making the *Briha*'s work extremely difficult. Bribes have to be increased to compensate for increased risks. There are serious delays, putting the entire operation in jeopardy. My task of keeping up the morale of the refugees and their hosts is more harrowing.

In December and January a new wave of refugees reaches our borders. Jews are now fleeing by the thousands from Hungary, where a radical Communist takeover has created havoc. Fearing that even the illegal escape routes would soon close, they leave behind all possessions and flee across the border into Czechoslovakia. Many Jewish refugees invariably find their way to *Briha* contacts and eventually wind up in Bratislava. How will *Briha* raise the enormous funds needed to accommodate the refugees during their stay in Bratislava? Sooner or later the underground railroad machinery will break down. What will happen to the refugees?

In January the Home receives orders from Zionist headquarters to prepare for a transport in ten days. Ten days! The excitement is indescribable. The girls are aflutter with preparation, packing, and good-byes. Ellike rushes downtown to buy an accordion as a present for Moshe, and I accompany her. Who knows when we will see each other again? Sori and Eva and Adele are jubilant. They have family members in Israel who anxiously await them. Malcah has corresponded with a childhood friend who has since become a prospective sweetheart. Judy and Valerie look forward to reuniting with their fiancés who left with illegal transports over a year ago. The dormitory resembles a beehive.

What will happen to Mother and me? Can we join the transport? I contact the Zionist headquarters, and they put me in touch with Mr. Kafka, one of the organizers.

With "deep regret" Mr. Kafka declines to register Mommy. "This transport is to include only young people," Mr. Kafka explains. "If you wish to join, we'll be happy to put your name on the list."

"What about my mother?"

"Your mother will have to join a later transport."

"When will there be a transport for her?"

"Some time later."

I cannot leave Mommy behind. Together we will wait for a transport that will include her.

Longingly I watch the girls as they make ready for the journey. Sheindi is packing prayer books and small volumes of the Bible to distribute to the fighters. Both Deena and Gitta have received news that they are being adopted by relatives in Tel Aviv. The two young girls have become inseparable during the last few months and now discover that their adoptive families live in the same Tel Aviv neighborhood. They are delirious with joy: Their future togetherness is ensured. Rachel, Zippora, Zivia, Pesi, Edit, Celia, Feigi, Libby, Layu, Chava, Zeesi, and Leah, and many others, have no relatives in Israel or anywhere else in the world. They have had nothing and no one. Now they will have a country to call their own. A land they have never seen awaits them.

The train to Vienna pulls up alongside the platform. A last embrace, a last word of farewell, and the train—its windows filled with frantically waving, cheering girls—moves out of the terminal with ever-increasing speed. Will I ever see them again?

I remain alone on the platform. Why is parting so painful? Why does my world collapse every time I say good-bye to people I love?

I think about my brother, separated from me not only by thousands of miles of ocean, but by an impenetrable Iron Curtain. I think about Mommy, now alone in Šamorín. What am I going to do now? The Beth Jacob School is finally closed. The last of my pupils, together with my closest friends, are on the train that is disappearing into the distant haze. The teachers' seminary, the English course at the Academy, Mrs. Gellert's dressmaker shop—are all things of the past.

The dormitory, Svoradova 7, is nearly deserted. Eight people instead of seventy occupy three spacious floors. Mrs. Meisels, the cook, was excluded from this transport because of her age. She occupies her previous private room downstairs near the kitchen. Miriam and her mother have moved into Malkele's room near the office on the second floor. Five girls live upstairs, in the two large dormitory rooms. Martha is waiting for the arrival of adoption papers from her uncle in America. "How will you get to America? There is no American embassy in this country to grant you a visa."

"My uncle will find a way to get me out," she says with absurd confidence. Emma, who recently received news that her father was alive in a Russian prison camp, has stayed behind to find ways of contacting him. Bozsi is determined to find a way to reach her brother in a Displaced Persons Camp in Germany. Lilli returned from a TB sanatorium in the Tatras too late to join the transport. Her cousins in Liberec have invited her to come there and share their plans for the future.

And then there is me.

I, unlike the others, have no clear-cut strategy. I am here by default. And I feel hopelessly trapped.

What will happen to us, Mommy and me? A disturbing conviction grows in my mind: I must engineer our escape before it is too late.

Mommy is now spending every Sabbath, and often a number of weekdays, with me in the Home to avoid exposure to the bitter cold in Šamorín. Our fuel supply has run out.

One particularly bitter night, when I return to the dormitory after escorting a group of Hungarian refugees to their quarters, I notice a narrow streak of light under Mommy's door.

At that moment I make a drastic decision: I must reveal my plan to Mommy.

Mommy is startled to see me. "You're still awake? Why is your nose so red? Were you outdoors? At this hour?"

Until now, whenever she stayed in the Home, I would kiss Mommy good night and then pretend to go to my room. Then I would slip out of the building to run my errands for the *Briha*.

It's almost three A.M. Mommy is a poor sleeper, but I never realized she stays awake this late. "And you, Mommy? What are you doing up at this hour?"

"I was thinking about Bubi," she explains. "In March it will be two years since he left, and there is still no prospect for our departure. No prospect at all. In his last letter he wrote that he contacted several U.S. congressmen, and next he will contact a senator, but he does not sound hopeful. I'm afraid he knows more about the gravity of our situation here than we do. His letter is very gloomy."

"That's the reason I've come to talk to you, Mommy. We know here, too, that the situation is worsening. The borders are getting tighter. More and more escape operations have to be devised for refugees from Poland and Hungary, and they are breaking down with increasing frequency. Last week a transport was intercepted, two women were shot and wounded. The entire transport was shipped back to Hungary. You can imagine what fate awaits them there."

"How do you know all this?"

"Mommy, I have been working with the *Briha*." Mommy's eyes open wide with alarm, and I go on before she can make a response. "I'm telling you all this because I have a plan. I've thought about this for a long time. We cannot wait any longer. We must join the next transport, you and I, to Vienna. And from there we'll make our way to America, somehow. The first priority is to get out of Czechoslovakia before it's too late.

"It has to be kept secret, even from our closest friends. You see, the *Briha* operates only for foreign refugees in transit. Under no circumstances are Czechoslovak citizens to join the transport. If they discover us among the refugees, my own colleagues would hand us over to the authorities, in order to save the operation. We must masquerade as Hungarians. We must invent Hungarian identities—names, places of birth, and a foolproof story of escape through the Hungarian border. I can invent such identities for both of us. I've heard enough tales working as interpreter for the investigating authorities. We both speak Hungarian like natives and know some Hungarian towns well enough to give a credible description of a birthplace or places of transit.

"No one must be aware of our plan. The people I work with must not realize we are there as refugees. They must think I brought you along to help out. God knows the *Briha* needs extra help. If they discover us among the refugees just before the transport is ready to leave, I don't suppose they would betray us. At that point, rather than jeopardize the transport, they would let us slip through. God forbid that we should be discovered."

Mommy is very thoughtful. "God forbid," she echoes. After a long pause, she says in a whisper, "My daughter, I'm afraid your plan is too daring. Too risky."

"I'm afraid we have no choice."

"We must think about it. We must think this out very carefully. I wish we could discuss it with someone."

"Mommy, there's no time to think. And there is no one we can trust to discuss it with. The next transport may be the last."

"When is the next transport?"

"I don't know. It may leave in a few days. It may also leave tomorrow."

"Tomorrow? When? What time?"

"The screening is being done during the night. Slovak military police interrogate every refugee, one by one, then hand him or her a pass. With these passes the refugees are loaded on trucks. As the trucks fill, they take off for the border. If a transport leaves tomorrow, I will be notified early in the evening. Then we will sneak into the old Jewish school building where the screening takes place. This is my normal routine. I escort refugees from their hideouts to the screening places."

"Tomorrow? That's impossible."

"Mommy, there's no time. I am afraid this is our last chance. If we miss this opportunity, we may never get out."

The Transport Is in Jeopardy

Bratislava, January—March 1949

Today frightening news reaches the *Briha* headquarters. Emil's face is grim as he begins his report: "I regret to inform you of a critical development."

"What's happened?" several volunteers ask at once.

"After crossing the Austrian border and reaching the Russian zone, border policemen came upon the convoy of vehicles and sprayed them with bullets before asking questions. Two refugees were killed, and several were wounded."

"Weren't the police paid to look the other way?"

"No one knows how it happened. There might have been a slipup, an unexpected change of guards at the last minute. The authorities claim it was a . . ." Emil falls silent.

"Please go on," we all urge him. "We want to know all the details."

"I believe it was a deliberate 'misunderstanding,' in line with the latest Slovak attitudes."

"What became of the refugees?"

"They were returned to Poland. Most were children who had been hidden in a Christian orphanage during the war. They were being transported under the auspices of the Youth Aliyah to Israel."

"Were any of the children hurt . . . or killed?"

"I don't know. We don't know the identities of the casualties, or of the injured. The border police did not allow any of our men even to approach them. The situation is changing rapidly. Our hands are virtually tied."

"What about the next transport?" someone ventures.

"It is uncertain when, and how. We will be in touch with you all. We'll let you know." Emil sounds ominous. I shudder at the thought of being caught. If the border police do not shoot me, Emil and the others will.

Mommy returns to Šamorín to settle our affairs. She manages to sell both houses, Aunt Serena's and ours, for ridiculously low prices.

However, it's fortunate that she succeeds in selling them at all. Private property transaction, or ownership, is a thing of the past. Everything has been nationalized. A local resident who secretly believes the Communist regime will eventually fall and he will end up a prosperous property owner has talked Mommy into the illicit sale. We need every penny we can raise. Our future is uncertain. Even if we make it to Vienna, we don't know how long we will have to linger there before proceeding to the United States.

Now that we have the cash, we have to devise a means of smuggling it out of the country. Dollars are your best bet, we are told.

"I've heard that Donny D., Bubi's former schoolmate, sells dollars on the black market. I'll go to see him," I tell Mommy.

The next morning I arrive at Donny's house carrying the large bundle of Czechoslovak bank notes, one hundred and ninety thousand crowns, in a briefcase.

"This amounts to fifty-seven dollars," Donny declares after extensive counting and calculation. "One five- and one ten-dollar bill, two twenty-dollar bills, and two single bills. Six bills altogether."

"That's all? How is that possible? All this money is worth only fifty-seven dollars?" I am in shock. "The price of two houses?"

"Look," Donny explains, "the crown has a very low value. Converted to black-market dollars it does not amount to much. If you were to purchase the dollars in smaller denominations, I can give them to you at a much higher rate of exchange."

"How much higher?"

"Let's see. If you accept small denominations, let's say one-dollar bills, I can give you sixty-six dollars."

Sixty-six, instead of fifty-seven, sounds like a good deal. And Donny assures me that the smaller denominations have the very same value in America as the larger bank notes. As a matter of fact, it is better to have smaller notes in America. They are easier to spend. Most places refuse to accept large notes.

I am happy with my purchase. Now I am the proud possessor of sixty-six dollars. A fortune. My very first American money. There is only one thought that gives me pause: Why are small notes that much cheaper? There has to be a good reason.

* * * *

Almost two months pass, and no transport. The wait gives Mommy and me ample time to prepare, and take every precaution against a slipup. Every shred of evidence of Slovak identity has to be destroyed. All my notebooks, letters, poems, and books written in Slovak have to be eliminated. Every label and stamp identifying the manufacturer has to be removed.

With a fine-tooth comb I sift through every item in our possession, and ink out signs of the most indirect association with local people. With trembling fingers I tear up every letter and note, some of profoundly sentimental value. With incisive pain I obliterate messages of affection from friends, pupils, and family members on the backs of photographs and on the title pages of books.

A deliberate violation of the self. Annihilation of identity. Canceling out the past.

This self-immolation by destroying personal papers is eerily reminiscent of the bonfire in which the Nazis burned our books, documents, pictures—paper of all kind—just before our deportation to Auschwitz. That bonfire was meant to destroy our past and our future. By burning every bit of paper, the Nazis attempted to destroy our soul. They meant to eliminate every trace of our having lived.

They did not succeed.

Once again we are pulling up our roots and obliterating our identity.

This time, in order to live.

How many more desperate acts of self-rape will we have to commit before we can reach a safe haven? Before we find a home where we can live free and be whole once again?

The "Screening"

The streets are enveloped in deep shadows, even though it is not yet five o'clock. As I turn onto Palisadna Street after my religion classes at the public school, a relentless wind slaps needle-sharp bits of frost into my face.

Life in Bratislava is dismal and dreary nowadays. The oppressive measures of the regime have taken a heavy toll on the atmosphere of this lovely city. People walk on the street with heads hanging, barely greeting each other.

From *Briha* headquarters there is no news about a transport. How much longer will we linger here in this prison? Every passing day jeopardizes our chances of escape.

At the entrance of the Home I meet Miriam bundled up in her mother's black coat with the fox collar.

"Someone's waiting for you in the lobby," she says with a wink. "He is not bad."

It's Shlomo, one of the *Briha* operatives.

"You are asked to report to headquarters immediately," Shlomo says under his breath.

"Is something wrong?"

Shlomo is noncommittal. "You're expected to accompany me. Can you come now?"

"Yes, of course."

We walk in swirling snowflakes. The electric streetcar makes too much of a detour; it is quicker to walk. The savage wind seems intent on penetrating my very soul. I shiver incessantly as I keep pace with Shlomo's rapid gait.

Pan Bloch and all the others are crowded in the tiny Briha office. Tension is tangible in the air. A transport is in the works, to be dispatched tomorrow night. The largest transport ever. The screening must start early tomorrow morning to prepare for the transport's takeoff by nightfall. The full cooperation of every member of the task force is required.

Pan Bloch turns to me: "Slečna Friedmannova. Your presence is essential." He stresses every word. "The transport is comprised mostly of Hungarians. We need you. I expect you to be there."

I feel my heart beat in my throat. This is our chance. I am going to be there—with Mommy. God forgive me. This time I'm going not to work for the *Briha* but to let the *Briha* work for me. I know I am committing betrayal on a grand scale. I know I'm putting my colleagues at risk. But I also know I have no alternative.

I gallop through the dark streets. Mommy has to be told immediately—it's tomorrow morning! We must pack at once. We must devise a way to sneak unnoticed into the school building.

When she gets the news, Mommy is seized by doubt.

"Are we doing the right thing? It's a rash decision, Elli, and much too risky. We may be discovered right at the start. And what a disaster that would be! Don't you think it's an altogether . . . irresponsible step?"

"Yes, I agree." I'm trying to keep self-recrimination, unendurable tension, and sheer panic out of my voice. "I agree with all you say, Mommy. But we have no alternative. This may be the last transport. It probably will be."

Can Mommy see the desperate appeal in my look? "Mommy, we have no choice. We have no money to bribe our way out of here privately. We are stuck. We may never see Bubi again."

Mommy is silent and very sad, and I know that she is going to pack as quickly and efficiently as no other human. She is the most competent person on earth.

"Mommy, I must run. I must alert my refugee groups and escort them to the gathering point in the school basement. They must spend the night there in preparation for early screening. I'll be back as soon as I can."

With a heart full of pain and apprehension, I accomplish my *Briha* assignment for the last time. When I return, Mommy is ready, just as I thought. Two neatly packed suitcases and backpacks are waiting near Mommy's bed in the little room. They contain all our worldly possessions. Mommy sewed two money belts out of ripped-up pillowcases to hold the dollar bills I have purchased. We divide the dollar notes evenly between the two of us and start stuffing them into the belt pockets. The sheer bulk of the bills makes the task nearly impossible. Now, belatedly, I understand why the single dollar bills were so much cheaper.

"There is simply no room in the money belt for all these bills!" Mommy is exasperated.

"Just try, Mommy, please. We must." When we finally accomplish the Herculean chore and strap the belts around our waists under our clothes, we look eight months pregnant.

"But this is impossible! We can't walk around like this!" By now Mommy is desperate. "Elli, I wish for once you'd spared us from one of your bargains!"

"Our coats will conceal the bulge. We'll keep our coats on."

Before retiring, Mommy and I take a casual leave from the dormitory residents. They understand we are preparing to spend a few days in Šamorín.

On the spur of the moment I confide in Miriam, and she gives me a quick, fierce, wordless embrace.

Next dawn Mommy and I walk with feigned calm to the school building where the screening is in progress. I assume my practiced stance, pretending to escort a refugee. I lead Mommy through the entrance to the first checkpoint in the corridor, which only refugees who passed the first screening can reach. Here the stern-faced Slovak officer in charge blocks our advance. But I hand him two slips of paper I have prepared in advance with our names in red. I hold my breath. The officer casts a curt glance at the slips of paper and, without looking either at Mommy or myself, directs us up the stairs to the main hall. Thank God. I resume breathing. Once upstairs it will be easier to dissolve in the crowd. Please God, let us not be apprehended. Help us, for our sake, and for the sake of the others. Let us all reach our destination without mishap, please.

The main hall is buzzing with a throng of humanity. It is an enormous transport. Just as I lead Mommy into the thick of the crowd, I notice Mr. Weise, Mr. Block, Emil, Eric, and Shlomo. I knew all the members would be here tonight. If any one of them sees me now, he is going to assume I am here to work, and without a second thought will address me in Slovak. That would give me away instantly. It would be the end. How can I avoid being spotted?

The toilet! I must hide in the toilet. All my fellow workers are men—they are not going to enter the women's toilet.

"Mommy," I whisper in Hungarian, "I will hide in the ladies' room. Call for me there when our turn comes."

Over two hours pass. Finally I hear a knock on the door, our prearranged signal. This is it. God, help us. Let the screening officer ask questions we can answer. I slip out of the toilet and join Mommy. Together we hurry down the corridor to the last door on the left.

It is a large, bare room with two large butcher-block tables. Behind one of them sit two dour civilians and a policeman with a somewhat friendlier face. The two civilians seem outright hostile. Mommy and I have decided to assume the identities of Hungarian relatives who perished in the Holocaust. Mommy is Aunt Perl, and I am her daughter Chavi. Now, while we face these stern-faced interrogators, we must concentrate hard on our new vital statistics.

The interrogators seem to assume that we

are guilty: Our every reply is greeted with a skeptical retort. I must try to ignore the belligerent line of questioning and doggedly, calmly stick to my story. I wish I could tell Mommy to do the same. How I wish I could give her a signal of encouragement. She looks panic-stricken. And very pale. Her voice has risen to an unnaturally high pitch. I hear her interrogator repeat his question.

"You say you were born in Sátoraljaújhely. Where did you live after your marriage?"

"In Sátoraljaújhely. I told you, I've always lived in Sátoraljaújhely."

"Always?" His eyebrows shoot up. "Always? You said you were in concentration camps. Were these camps also in Sátoraljaújhely?"

"No, of course not. They were in Poland and in Germany."

"Ah, so you did not *always* live in Sátoraljaújhely. You also lived in Poland and Germany."

"No! I never lived in Poland and Germany!" Mommy shouts indignantly. Mommy is getting angry. That's dangerous. In her anger I hope she's not going to say anything that will give us away. God, help us. "I was in the camps there. That was not living. That was barely existing."

"Is that so?" The civilian's voice is dripping with venom. "Ah, and in Sátoraljaújhely, how long did you live there, excluding the time you 'existed' in Poland and Germany?"

"All my life. Up to three weeks ago."

"All your life? And how long has that been?"

"I told you, fifty. I'm fifty years old. But I have told you that already!"

"Ah, is that so? Now . . . let's see. If you're fifty years old, you lived in Sátoraljaújhely for only forty-nine years. Isn't that so?"

"Yes."

"Ah, so why do you say fifty, eh?" If looks could kill, Mommy would fall lifeless to the floor from the look the interrogator now shoots at her. "Let's proceed, and see if you can give me accurate answers. If you lived in Sátoraljaújhely for forty-nine years, you'd say you know the town well, wouldn't you?"

"Pretty well, yes. I know Sátoraljaújhely pretty well."

"Then you'd know the name of the river that runs through the city, would you not? The river that cuts the city in half, what is it called?"

My God, is there a river in Sátoraljaújhely? I've never heard of it. I'm sure Mommy hasn't, either. What will she say?

"It's not a river." Mommy is lying. "It's only a stream."

"Is that so? In that case, what's the name of the stream?"

"It has no real name. We just call it 'The Stream.' In Sárospatak, that's a town nearby, they call it 'Muddy Stream,' Sáros Patak. That's how the town derived its name. But we just called it 'The Stream.'" I'm dying. I know this is the end. Mommy's little performance about the nonexistent stream with the nonexistent name is to be our epitaph. And of the entire transport. I'm about to close my eyes, ready for the end, when suddenly the nasty civilian turns to me, speaking Slovak.

"*Slečna*, why should we bother talking Hungarian? State your full name, please."

I stare as if I am deaf. Now he addresses me in a friendlier tone: "Miss, what's your name, please?"

I pretend to look puzzled. "Excuse me, sir. Are you talking to me?"

He looks down at his notes on the table

and repeats the question, now in Hungarian. Silently I sigh a secret sigh of relief. Now both men proceed shooting questions at me in rapid succession about my age, birthplace, schooling, then snap their folders shut. The policeman hands us two slips of paper, and with these we are to proceed to the customs checkup. The screening is over.

My eyelids and legs feel like lead . . . and I am walking submerged in a murky whirlpool. I have difficulty finding my way out of the room and down the crowded corridor. Mommy is holding on to my arm, and it feels as if I am dragging her like ballast against the current.

Now we wait on line for our names to be called for customs inspection. Suddenly, overwhelmingly, it penetrates my consciousness: We've made it! Thank God, we've made it!

Almost.

All of a sudden, I hear a familiar voice right behind me.

"Slečna Friedmannova. Here you are. I was looking all over for you." It is Shlomo's voice. Instantly I realize I must not respond. Not to anyone addressing me in Slovak. I stifle an impulse to turn my head, and remain motion-less, staring ahead. How I have prayed and hoped against hope that something like this should not transpire.

Shlomo comes around to face me: "Elli, what are you doing here? Emil needs you at the screening. We need a Hungarian inter-preter urgently."

I cannot avoid Shlomo's gaze. Without moving a facial muscle I stare into his eyes and say slowly, deliberately, in Hungarian: "Sir, there must be a mistake. I do not speak Slovak."

Shlomo's eyes open wide with shock. His mouth is agape but does not utter a sound. At that very instant, our names are called, and Mommy reaches for her suitcase. Without removing his gaze from my face, Shlomo reaches for Mommy's suitcase.

"May I help you, madam?" I feel blood rush into my face as I follow Mommy and Shlomo with the rest of the luggage into the auditorium to join the long lines for the lug-gage to be inspected. Mortified, I avert my eyes while Shlomo abruptly vanishes in the crowd. After arranging the luggage, I make my way to join Mommy on line. The next instant, I find myself face-to-face with Emil!

Emil's face brightens: "Elli, you're here?" he asks, somewhat puzzled. As a volunteer I am not supposed to be in this auditorium. My task is in the hall where the screening takes place. Yet, he is obviously glad to have found me. "Great. I need you badly," he says with a preoccupied smile. When he notices my lack of response, Emil looks searchingly into my face. I return his gaze with a blank expression, and in a flash he realizes. His eyes scan my face with a mixture of shock and embarrassment, and his complexion turns scarlet.

Then he addresses me in halting Hungarian with a thick Slovak accent: "I'm sorry, miss. I mistook you for someone else. This way." He picks up the two largest pieces of luggage. "Come, there are much shorter lines over there."

Mommy and I follow Emil through the noisy crowd. Suddenly he turns and bends close to my ear. I can barely make out his words above the din.

"Are you sure you know what you're doing?"

"We passed screening. Everything is okay."

"How *could* you? Especially *you?*"

"I had no alternative."

Emil does not answer until we reach a line made up of only three people. "Here we are, miss," he says in an official tone. "I wish you and your mother a successful journey."

I read Emil's face and see that the farewell is genuine, and it is meant for me, the colleague with whom he shared long hours of harrowing work for over a year. It took charity and courage for Emil to say those words. No one knows better than I the gravity of the offense that I have committed. No one knows better than I the generosity of spirit Emil has just displayed in giving me, at the last moment, a gracious send-off.

At the Border

March 8, 1949

We must be approaching the border. The convoy has been on the road for over an hour, most of the time traversing long stretches of wooded terrain. The canvas flaps of the truck keep out the fierce wind, but the wind's cold edge seems to filter through and chill me to the bone. I feel like a deflated balloon. I'm relieved, hurt, and frightened, all at the same time.

Thank God we made it through screening without putting ourselves and the *Briha* in jeopardy. However, one of our suitcases was confiscated by customs. It contained our most valuable things: a crystal vase, tapestry wall hangings, bedspreads, a silver candelabra, embroidered and lace tablecloths. These items were especially dear to me: They were among the things we recovered from our Gentile neighbors after our return from the concentration camps. The customs inspectors claimed they were manufactured in Czechoslovakia and must not leave the country.

My native land's brutal gesture of farewell feels like the ultimate irony. First I was robbed by the Nazis. And now by their sworn adversaries—the Communists. How much injustice can you absorb before you lose your sense of self?

A hair-raising hurdle still awaits us—the border, and beyond. God, save us. It was here that the last convoy, in January, was detected and sprayed with machine-gun fire. God, help us reach Vienna and the American Zone.

The trucks come to a halt, and we are told to disembark. In the forest clearing, an endless row of huge camouflaged trucks awaits us. The enormous vehicles strung with pine branches at odd angles, and guarded by armed drivers, present a scary, grotesque sight. I tighten my grip on my backpack. A sense of danger tightens the pit of my stomach. We are about to cross into the Russian Zone.

There are so many trucks, I am unable to count them. The transfer proceeds in total silence at lighting speed. I am unable to guess at the numbers of people being transferred in the dark, thick forest. What an amazingly efficient operation! The expert *Briha* team, under the direction of a towering figure in a black pea jacket, is proceeding like clock-work.

The *Briha* commander now turns sideways, and I recognize him. My God! It's him . . . it's Vilo.

Vilo Grentze, a *Briha* commander? I must be hallucinating.

"Mommy!" I whisper in her ear, and almost choke with excitement. "Can you see that tall man in the black jacket, giving orders? Now he's facing the other way. Can you see him?" I grasp Mommy's arm for support. "Do you know who that is? He's the guy I told you about, at the road construction last winter. . . ."

"Of course, I remember well."

"It's him! The Communist whose mother was a Jew, and his father, a German. . . ."

All at once Vilo turns around, facing us. In the next instant he stands before me. "Elli Friedmannova!" He places both hands on my shoulders. His beaming face is inches away from mine. "Elli Friedmannova. They told me you're working with us. How have you been? How have you been?"

"Thank you, fine. Thank God . . . I . . ." I lower my voice to a whisper. "I'm . . . in the transport . . . not on an assignment . . ."

Vilo's eyebrows shoot up, and he instantly checks himself. His next question stops in midair. I put my arm about Mommy's shoulders. "Vilo, meet my mother." I switch to Hungarian. "Mother and I are heading for Vienna."

Vilo shakes his head and whispers in Slovak, "I don't speak Magyar."

"I'm sorry. I didn't know."

"No need to apologize, Elli. Where to? America? Palestina?"

"I don't know . . . We'll see what happens in Vienna. . . ."

He takes my hands into his and speaks in a voice so low, I have to bring my ear near his lips to hear: "Good thing you got out of Bratislava. The transports will terminate very soon. . . . When?" He shrugs his shoulders. "No one knows for sure."

"And you, Vilo. Will you go to Palestina?"

"Perhaps someday. Now the Party needs me. Someday I'll get there. *Naša svetá zem . . .* Remember?" A mischievous smile lights up his brilliant eyes. Strange. Once I thought they were small and piercing. "*Nazdar*, Elli." Vilo draws my face near and plants a kiss on my cheek. Oh, God, right in front of Mommy! Then he extends his hand to Mommy. "*Zbohom*, Pani Friedmannova." Good-bye, Mrs. Friedmann. Then with a wink he adds, "*Dovidenia!*" See you again! And hurries back to his post.

All of a sudden I am conscious of my appearance. What am I wearing? Thank God. The olive-green coat and gray felt boots, the latest fashion. We could take only one change of clothing, so naturally we chose our best pieces to wear. What a relief! Vilo has seen me in my good coat.

Vilo is directing the entire operation. He does not see me climb in the truck right behind Mommy. The interior of this truck is even icier than the first. The canvas covering has a long gash right near my seat, and the inexorable wind assaults every part of my body without restraint.

I recognize Vilo's voice nearby singing out,

"*Čislo devat. Odchod!*" Number nine. Depart!

That's us. We are about to take off. As the engine revs, the canvas flaps open slightly at the front end and Vilo's face appears in the gap: "Elli Friedmannova!"

"*Tu som!*" Here I am! I call out from my corner seat in the back of the truck.

Vilo waves an arm into the shadowy interior. "*Lehitraot B'Tel Aviv. Lehitraot B'Eretz Yisrael.*" See you again in Tel Aviv. See you in the Land of Israel. I cannot believe my ears. In Hebrew? Vilo, the Communist official. Vilo the *Briha* commander. And now, Vilo the Zionist?

"*Lehitraot,*" I shout as the truck begins to move and Vilo's face is obliterated by canvas or by darkness. I am afraid Vilo has not heard me. My voice betrayed me at the crucial moment of parting from Vilo Grentze. My throat is dry, and I feel faint. Mommy touches my hand. "Don't cry, Elli. Everything will work out fine. God will help us. One day you'll meet him again."

Freedom at Last

Vienna, March 8, 1949

Suddenly the trucks' headlights are turned off, plunging the forest into darkness. Picking their way blindly among myriad trees and murky foliage, the vehicles inch along as unobtrusively as a herd of elephants.

I huddle close to Mother. I cannot see her face, but her hands are as cold as ice. I keep shivering and dozing, and Mommy keeps urging me to eat. Minutes before leaving Mommy managed to pack food for our journey. My stomach protests. I find even breathing difficult.

Silence envelops the dark forest like a lush blanket. All at once even the trucks' engines are shut off, and the camouflaged vehicles float downhill like phantoms. Our drivers' uncanny ability to navigate the woods from Bratislava through the Russian Zone to Vienna in total darkness is the key to this secret escape route.

There is a sudden burst of machine-gun fire in the distance. But we are beyond its range. The truck moves somewhat faster now. Minutes later the ignition and headlights turn on, and we burst into spontaneous applause.

"Silence, comrades," the driver warns. "We're not out of danger yet."

But I can tell there is a smile in his voice. I begin to weep. Mother weeps, too, soundlessly; only her hands tremble. The vehicles drive fast now, and within minutes we are on the open road. A young comrade begins to sing, and we all join in: *"Hevenu shalom aleikhem . . .* We bring you greetings of peace."

I peek through the gash in the canvas next to my seat. It is quiet out there. No machine-gun fire, no shouting. We have made it. Dark buildings materialize out of the fog. I see city lights! We are rolling on the streets of Vienna.

Vienna of the "Blue Danube," of Strauss's waltzes, of whipped-cream cakes. Vienna, the port of refugee dreams. The island of freedom.

We are heading for an abandoned Jewish hospital named after the Rothschilds. It is now a collection center for refugees. This old ramshackle building, jam-packed with countless refugees, is going to be our home.

Which corner of the Rothschild Hospital will be allotted to Mommy and me? Will we have to fight for a bed, a blanket? Where will we put our belongings? How many refugees for one toilet? For a shower? I am very tired. I no longer want to struggle. An involuntary shudder passes through my body.

Mommy says, "I hope you're not coming down with a cold. Just when we are heading for an unknown destination! If only you'd eat properly."

The caravan rolls through an open gate and comes to a halt in the middle of a yard. The truck's canvas covering flips open and unveils a drab, wet backyard cluttered with wooden crates and parked army trucks. Crowds of people emerge from the dark drizzle and approach the vehicles. Names are called, greetings are shouted in a medley of languages— Hungarian, Polish, Yiddish. There are people among us who are awaited by friends.

"Boys, look!" someone shouts. "Look who is here! The girl from Bratislava. Can you believe this? Here she is. Look!" I am blinded by a flashlight trained into my face. Hands reach for our suitcase. Hands lift me off the truck and place me gently on the wet ground. "Welcome! Welcome to Vienna, girl from Bratislava. Isn't it wonderful? This way, boys. Here she is! Can you ever believe it?"

What's going on? Who are these boys? "Would you help my mother, please?" I call into the dark beyond the blinding light. "Mommy, this way . . ." They reach for Mommy and lift her off the truck. "Please . . . I cannot see. Your flashlight. Would you turn it off?" Mercifully, the flashlight is lowered, and out of the darkness I start to distinguish seven or eight young men. I recognize them now. "You were in Bratislava several weeks ago."

"Hey, boys! The girl from Bratislava remembers us." A fellow with wavy blond hair, his face lit up with a brilliant grin, extends a hand: "Welcome to Vienna!" A tall, lanky young man declares with ceremony, "Welcome to freedom." And then, one by one, each shakes my hand firmly and offers words of greeting with a beaming face.

Now I remember them well. About two

months ago they spent ten or eleven days in our transit camp. I was assigned to supply their immediate needs. Before their departure they vowed, "Whenever you arrive in Eretz Israel, we'll carry you on a silver platter." Who was to know that we would meet much, much sooner, in Vienna?

The boys carry our suitcase and lead us like trophies of war in a procession through the crowded hallways of the hospital. We reach an enormous, brightly lit ward lined with beds and metal cabinets. Blankets in various colors and patterns are hung around the beds on strings that stretch from wall to wall. Luggage is piled high in the center of the room. The beds are flanked by narrow school benches, baby carriages, and ornate cradles. People of every age, shape, and color fill all available space. This must be the most crowded, the most colorful hospital ward on record.

At one table a lively card game is going on. At another, a woman is feeding a baby and peeling potatoes at the same time. At the same table a man is absorbed in writing. At a third, there is a discussion going on, feverish, compelling. It is a dynamic, optimistic scene.

My fear and fatigue are long gone. The boys' friendly reception and this ward's festive welcome has dispelled all doubt about our future in Vienna. And beyond.

The boys lead us to two empty beds in the corner, then bring sheets and pillowcases and help make the beds. One whips the old blankets off the beds and drapes them over the string, magically transforming the corner into a private bedroom for Mommy and me. Then they all go scouting for new blankets and towels.

"Here, ladies. The royal suite is ready." The boys beam with delight, and I, indeed, feel like royalty in our new home.

"It's almost ten. At ten sharp the lights go out," the boys warn.

"Let me show you to the washrooms," the tall, lanky one volunteers, and all the others join the expedition. Near the washroom entrance, they all take their leave. They must hurry to their room on the second floor before lights out.

"Good night, girl from Bratislava. Tomorrow we'll introduce you to Vienna."

Spring in Vienna

March—September 1949

"Good morning!" Mommy's face is aglow
with happiness. "How did you sleep?" Without waiting for an answer, Mommy goes on,
almost breathlessly, "I slept like a log. And
look, Elli. The boys brought all this!"

The hospital ward is illuminated by brilliant
morning sun. All blankets are drawn open, and
I am hurled onto the live stage of an amazing
planet in perpetual motion. At the foot of our
bed is a school desk with two benches at either
side. The desktop is covered with metal plates
heaped with rolls and large chunks of butter.
From two large metal mugs the aroma of fresh-
brewed coffee wafts into the air.

"And here's some Austrian money, two
hundred shillings. We can go out and buy
anything we need. The boys say there are all
kinds of fabulous shops in the vicinity."

"Mommy, this is Paradise. Would you have thought that it was going to turn out like this?"

"These boys were sent by God. And they are so handsome, so full of life. So full of charm. What would we do without them?" Charm is a top rating in Mother's vocabulary.

"Mommy, I believe we are going to be happy here!"

"You can't be happy just lolling in bed. Get up quick, and let's have our breakfast while the coffee is hot. Here's a towel. The washroom is at the other end of the corridor."

Luckily I was too tired last night to unpack, and I slept in my house robe. Now all I have to do is hop out of bed and skip down the corridor to the bathroom. Life is simply marvelous. Last night's fog and drizzle have dissipated, and even the hallway is bathed in light.

On my way back from the bathroom, I meet the twins near the entrance to our room. All the boys had introduced themselves last night, and I took note of all their names. The twins are Andy and Tommy. The sturdy fellow with the wavy dark blond hair is Hayim.

The tall, lanky one with hazel eyes is Peter. The other tall young man, with wide shoulders and shiny black hair, is Leslie. And then there are Julius, a slim, wiry boy with light blond curls, and Stephan, a bespectacled charmer with a dimpled chin and brilliant dark eyes.

They are a close-knit group, friends since their kindergarten days in a small Hungarian village. Peter and Leslie are twenty-six years old; all the others are twenty-four. Together they survived forced labor camps in Hungary while their families perished in Auschwitz.

Andy is carrying a blue enamel pitcher of steaming milk.

"For your first breakfast in Vienna," he says.

"What a charming milk maid! Thank you. Where does the milk come from?"

"I get special privileges in the community kitchen. The cook likes me. She's a Pollack, and like all Pollacks, hates Hungarians. But she says I'm different. I'm not like a Hungarian. So here it is, a token of her love."

"So that's how the luscious rolls and butter and mugs of fresh-brewed coffee got here! Long live your charms, Andy!"

"What rolls and coffee?"

Tommy winks at me conspiratorially behind his brother's back. I remember the twins' ongoing rivalry from Bratislava and hasten to do damage control by quickly changing the subject. "Andy, thank you so much for the milk. It's so kind of you . . ."

But Mommy, who knows neither the twins nor anything about their relationship, politely explains, pointing at Tommy. "This young man here brought the splendid rolls and butter, and the coffee. For years I've not tasted butter and rolls like these. And the aroma of that coffee! It's the lap of luxury to have such breakfast. What a marvelous welcome to Vienna. We are truly grateful for your kindness. . . ."

As Mommy speaks, Andy turns scarlet and Tommy's face is a study in glee. His eyes dance with mischief as he announces, feigning modesty, "Peter got the butter. We must give him credit for that. I managed only the coffee and the rolls."

Formally tipping his hat, Andy takes an abrupt leave. "*Bon appétit,* ladies," he says to Mommy and me, then turns to his brother:

"Let's go." He is three hours older than Tommy but has assumed the role of elder brother as if the difference were in years not hours.

Tommy obediently follows him. Near the exit he turns and gives us a wink with a grin as wide as the brim of his fedora.

After breakfast the entire gang appears to take us for a walk and show us the shops, the post office, and the nearest streetcar stop. Our camp is in the heart of a lively, bustling metropolis. As if the war had been a thousand years ago, Vienna is brimming with carefree vitality.

Actually, this is true only of the American Zone. At war's end the victorious powers— the Americans, the Russians, the British, and the French—divided Vienna into four zones, each occupying one. The British and French Zones are noticeably duller. These comprise the more outlying districts, and that may also account for their lack of luster and exuber- ance. The Russian Zone, although the largest district of the inner city, is dead. It reminds me of Bratislava after the Communist coup. Going from the American Zone to the Russian Zone is like watching a spirited young woman suddenly turn into a corpse. You feel as though you have walked backward through time and suddenly have entered a war zone. The ruins lie untouched. You walk past empty buildings, abandoned stores, piles of broken bricks and masonry heaped high at intersections. An atmosphere of gloom has wrapped itself around the neighborhood like a leaden shroud. And when you return to the American Zone, your pulse quickens again with the sheer joy of being alive.

Vienna is my oyster in the spring of 1949. I am eighteen, and six boys wait on my every whim. Leslie, the oldest, is engaged to be married. He does not join in our junkets. But the others—handsome, humorous, and bright—vie for my attention, each in his own inimical, fun-loving fashion. We rent bicycles, and six boys compete for a place by my side on our ride into the fabulous Viennese hills. One of the boys sketches the landscape and presents the sketch to me as a loving souvenir. Another writes poetry, poignant little love declarations. One plays the accordion, another one the flute, and the third, the harmonica—and I am serenaded day after day.

We ride on the Riesenrad in the Prater, and when we reach the top, the exhilarating high point of the giant wheel, six boys want to hold my hand. When we descend, six boys buy me little trinkets, little mementos of the adventure. We take boat rides on the Danube Canal, and six boys take turns rowing while we sing Strauss's "Blue Danube" waltz. We take pony rides in the gardens of the Schönbrunn Palace, and the six boys serve as my retinue. We go to the famous Vienna Opera and Burgtheater, and six furtively fix their gazes on me instead of the stage. I pretend not to notice, but from the corner of my eye I see it well. And I grow giddy with delight.

I love all six of them. There are no clouds on the horizon; Vienna remains eternally dazzling. The spring ripens into summer, but for me Vienna remains forever spring. The only carefree, joyful spring I have known.

The parks of the city, the banks of the Danube Canal, the forests on the outskirts, and the hills above are my playground. The fabulous Ring, and the Prater. The Burg. The museums. The Schönbrunn Palace. Vienna, elegant and grand, vivacious and charming, city of the Hapsburgs, of the Strausses and Liszt, your music and bewitching landscape, your freedom, has restored my soul.

And yet, you are the city that embraced Hitler with open arms—I shut my eyes and refuse to remember it. You shouted *"Juden raus"* and thundered *"Heil Hitler!"* even louder than Berlin—I plug my ears and refuse to hear it. Your language is German, your face is Aryan, your soul is corrupt—I seal my mind and refuse to think.

For five months I blot out reality and indulge in delusion. For five months I exhilarate in undiluted youth.

I am eighteen in Vienna and do not yet know that I will never be eighteen again.

Andy

Vienna, May—June 1949

In time, Andy becomes a "special" friend. He is the first gang member to visit every morning and the last one to leave in the evening. On our walks, bicycle rides, and shopping trips, he monopolizes the space near me. He always snatches the seat next to me at the movies and at all the other places we attend, always conniving ways to be alone with me. Before I notice what is happening, the other gang members begin to keep their distance. This nonverbal "understanding" is at times challenged by Tommy or Pete. During Andy's visit Tommy would sometimes appear in our room, nonchalantly flicking his cigarette and, with mock formality, present me with a red rose. Andy would turn scarlet and stare at his brother with ferocious intensity but make no sound or movement until the latter tipped his hat and made his exit. A few minutes later Pete would appear and insinuate himself between Andy and me at the foot of the bed. Andy would fall silent again, awaiting the end of Peter's visit. But Pete would ignore Andy's discomfort and stay, invariably bringing up innocuous topics of discussion and causing Andy visible anguish. Sometimes the sunshine would beckon, and we would continue our chat in the park, where several other members of the gang would join us. Andy, his "territorial rights" violated, would bristle with annoyance and plunge into deep gloom.

Mommy is amused by these goings-on. She likes the boys and is tickled pink also with the little tokens of attention they shower on her as well. But lately she is concerned about Andy's growing intensity and warns me "not to encourage him."

Andy is intelligent and high-strung. He is the most serious and the most educated, and from the start has assumed a leadership position in the group.

I have not objected to this subtle arrangement, because I enjoy Andy's company and his erudite debates. I find his intensity strangely stimulating.

This afternoon, Andy seems more intense than usual.

"I received a telegram from my sister today," he reveals with obvious tension when we are sitting alone on a park bench. "She and her husband are due to arrive next Tuesday."

"How nice for you and your brothers! You must be very happy."

"Yes. Next Tuesday . . . that's in five days. It would make me very happy if I could introduce you to my sister. Will you permit me to introduce you . . ."

"Of course! What a question! Of course you may introduce me. I have been hoping to meet her. . . ."

All three brothers, Andy, Tommy, and Leslie, have been speaking about their elder sister with great affection and anxiously awaiting her arrival. I feel I have gotten to know Annie through the brothers' references to her warmth and sense of humor. Andy's attachment to her and his anxious waiting for the young couple's arrival have made me especially eager to meet her.

"No . . . not that—" Andy nervously interrupts. "I wish to. . . may I introduce you . . . as my fiancée?"

Even I can hear my sudden intake of breath. I am thunderstruck. Is this a marriage proposal?

I have always wondered how it would happen. Who would it be? What would he say? Under what circumstances? So that's how it happens. Out of the clear blue. Just like that. "Introduce you as my fiancée." Andy did not say he wished to marry me. Or that he loved me. He simply wanted to introduce me as his fiancée. How strange.

"How can you introduce me as your fiancée when I'm not? I'm not your fiancée, Andy, am I?"

"What I meant was . . . would you? Would you be my fiancée? I love you very much. From the first moment. Since Bratislava . . . I have had no rest. Not a moment's rest. I've not slept for weeks, thinking of you . . . thinking of how to ask you to marry me. Thinking of what you'll say."

Now he's said it. He's said it all. Love. Marriage. Torment. Just as it is in the novels.

Just as I have imagined. How strange. I feel nothing. Not even flattered. On the contrary, I am embarrassed. Painfully embarrassed.

"Andy." I so wish to say the right words. *Are* there right words?

"Andy, you see, I don't know where I'm heading. There is so much I want to do. Most of all, I want to study. I don't know if I'll ever get to America, but if I do, I want to work by day and study at night. In America you can do that. I want to complete high school and then go to college. I don't know when I will get married. But it is not now. Not for a long time yet."

Andy is silent for a long time. His eyes are fixed on a cluster of bushes ahead. "I know," he says at long last. "I knew it all the time. If I were to go to America, if I were to live where you'll live, then perhaps in a year or two, when you are nineteen or twenty . . . maybe then you'd be ready to get married." Andy falls silent again. Is he expecting an answer? Now his intent gaze falls on the ground, where a few blades of grass have been flattened by the agitated tapping of his feet. "But . . . ," he goes on after a long pause, "I have no prospects of getting to America. And so, when you are ready to get married, I won't be there. You'll be in America, and I'll be in Israel."

What shall I answer? Shall I tell him that I would not marry him in Israel, either? Neither him nor anyone else. I want to achieve my goals first, and that will take years. One day I want to be a teacher in an institution of higher learning. I want to speak English with impeccable pronunciation. And write beautiful, literary English. I also want to extend my knowledge of Hebrew. Israel will be my home one day, and I want to know Hebrew as if it were my native tongue. I have no time for marriage. I never even think about marriage.

Andy is very, very quiet. In a barely audible tone he says he understands. He is not feeling very well, he admits. Would I mind if he went home? No, he does not want me to walk with him. Abruptly Andy mumbles good-bye and hurries away.

I do not understand what has happened. Didn't Andy say he understood? Then why the hasty departure?

I must have hurt him, after all. I will make up for it later. We have a date tonight: We are going to see *Der Fledermaus,* a very popular opera in Vienna. I am sure the music will lift his spirits. He has been looking forward to tonight. I will explain everything afterward. I'm sure he'll see my points then.

"I'll see you later!" I call after Andy. I don't know if he can hear me. He is just turning the corner and does not look back.

Andy is due to call for me at 5:10. At five I am ready. I am wearing my pink taffeta dress, the one I designed for the exam in my pattern-making course in Bratislava. It is a lovely two-piece dress with a flaired skirt, a tight waist, and a form-fitting top. The dolman sleeves and the Cossack-style standing collar lend it a striking, dramatic look. Andy likes this dress, and he will be pleased that I have chosen it for tonight. My hair is long, with a soft wave, the aftermath of a permanent wave that has, thankfully, grown out since then. The new shampoo I bought here in Vienna gives my hair a brilliant luster.

I am glad I look my best. Andy will be pleased, despite our little misunderstanding.

Or perhaps because of it. I will be very warm and attentive all evening. It is essential that he does not take my refusal to marry him personally. I must make amends whatever way I can.

It is 5:10, and Andy has not come. Normally he is very punctual. Five-thirty, and no Andy. Five forty-five comes and goes without Andy's appearance. I start to change into my ordinary clothes, all the while keeping an eye on the entrance to our room. Mommy is my official lookout. At six o'clock she advises me to go upstairs and find out what has happened to Andy. I categorically refuse. I know Andy is angry with me, and this is his way of punishing me. There is no point in swallowing my pride. I am not going to beg for forgiveness. I am sorry to have hurt his feelings. I am sorry to miss *Der Fledermaus*. And I am very sorry for not having had a chance to show off my fancy clothes. But to go to Andy's room and risk being snubbed in front of all the gang members? Never.

Around eight o'clock several of the gang members usually call. Tonight not one comes to visit. What's going on? If Andy was home, they would know I was home. Perhaps Andy is not at home. Where is he, then? Did he go to the opera by himself? Or, perhaps, with someone else? Would he do such a thing? It's not like him.

All evening no one comes, not even Peter. I am miserable.

"Why don't you go upstairs and investigate?" Mommy keeps urging. "I don't understand your mulish stubbornness."

Mommy does not know about the afternoon incident in the park. How can I expect her to understand my reluctance to humiliate myself in front of Andy and his friends?

In the morning Peter comes to visit. His behavior is strangely reserved. After some small talk he suddenly blurts out: "Elli, I'm sorry to tell you, but Andy is very ill."

"Andy? What are you talking about?"

"Late afternoon he came back from somewhere downcast and did not speak to anyone. Later in the evening he became agitated and confused. He started to talk irrationally. Then he began to shout. When we tried to calm him, he turned on us. He became violent. He threatened to kill Tommy, then tackled him and began to strangle him. It took four of us to pull him off and hold him while someone called the house police. The police called for an ambulance. He was so violent that he broke a male attendant's finger. The police had to tie him up. He was taken to a sanatorium in the Vienna woods. We all spent the night in the nearby woods and went to see him early this morning. He is asking for you. The boys sent me to give you the message and ask you to go see him."

Oh, God. My dear God.

"Where is he? Which sanatorium?"

"It's a state institution, in Semmering. About an hour's ride by bus from the Danube Canal terminal. Visiting hours begin at two o'clock. We are all going. Do you want to come along? He keeps asking for you."

"I'm so sorry. Andy and I had a misunderstanding yesterday."

"We all know about that. For days he was very nervous about talking to you. We all knew he was going to ask you to marry him. We all told him it was a hopeless case, but he wouldn't listen. He worked himself into a state."

"I am very sorry. I had no idea. . . ."

"Don't blame yourself. It's not your fault.

Do you think you want to come to the hospital? You don't have to. I can tell him you felt it was better that you saw him after he came out of the hospital."

"How is he? Is he rational?"

"Now he is less agitated and less confused. I think he is sedated. But he keeps repeating that he must talk to you."

"Thank you, Peter. I think I should go. Will you please call for me?"

Shortly after Peter leaves, Tommy comes to thank me for agreeing to go visit his brother.

"You're simply wonderful for doing this. It's a great *mitzvah*." I reject his accolades, and Tommy refuses to listen to my self-recriminations.

A few minutes later Leslie, the oldest brother, comes to warn me: "You should be prepared for a great change in my brother. He may be abusive. Please, think it over. You may not want to be exposed to this."

I thank Leslie for his concern. "I must go to see him. I'll be okay."

In the bus my stomach shrinks to a tiny, hard ball. I do not know what to expect. The gentle, soft-spoken, intelligent young man is in a mental ward for the violent. I cannot grasp it. I have a crushing sense of sadness and an overwhelming desire to do something to help Andy.

The bus stops in front of a sprawling yellow building with black wrought-iron gates. We walk on impeccably white gravel paths through a well-tended garden, up wide, stone stairs to the black metal doors. They are locked. We have to ring a bell, then another. A little window in the middle of the door opens. A face appears. Then the portal opens, and the cool, shadowy interior receives us silently. Locks click, and the gate shuts behind us.

"Second floor," the attendant replies to our inquiry. "To the right. To the end of the corridor."

White-clad attendants slip past soundlessly. We approach a narrow metal door with peeling white paint. Again we must press a doorbell, which prompts the opening of a peephole in the door, the flicker of an eye. We slip our visitors' passes into a slot under the peephole and are admitted to a small corridor. The lock clicks behind us, and we are facing another metal door with peeling white paint, bell, peephole, and attendant. Finally we enter a spacious room. The walls are lined with rows of mesh cages.

My legs are leaden. Tommy touches my arm: "This way, Elli." I allow myself to be led to the cage next to the last on the left wall. In the cage lies a human creature in a dark blue hospital uniform, with hair cropped to the scalp and two enormous dark eyes fixed on the ceiling in an unflinching gaze.

"Andy?" A faint flicker. A smile? No. A frightened shadow of a grin.

"He has recognized you," Leslie whispers. The frightened grin remains fixed, but the eyes continue their one-track stare. My God. Is this really Andy?

I place my palm against the metal mesh. "Andy? Andy?"

The eyes open wider. They become two black pools. The grin fades, and slowly a hand reaches toward the metal mesh and sweeps lightly the spot where my palm is flattened. Then the hand drops, and the eyes close. The face becomes the face of a corpse, drained of color and life.

I turn around to face the others. "He is tired. He is very tired." Their faces all have the same expression of bewilderment. "I think we should speak to a doctor or something. To find out why is he so . . . so tired."

Leslie speaks German best. "I will find a doctor," he volunteers. "Wait for me here."

We all move away from Andy's cage, as if afraid to wake him with our presence. The heavy silence turns each minute into an eternity. Finally Leslie returns.

"A nurse told me he received treatment this morning. An electric shock, or something. The treatment is draining."

I tiptoe to the mesh. Andy lies in a stupor, and the metal grating casts a curious shadow on his inert features. Please, God, is he dead? Will he ever be himself again?

"I think we should leave now. He is going to sleep." Leslie is in charge, and we are grateful. We need a guiding hand to cope with this shocking, incomprehensible reality.

We pass through a series of doors and locks on our way out of the building. The sun is shining, but the dark gloom of the hospital seems to follow us like a cloud all the way back to the colorful, noisy excitement of the Rothschild Hospital, our home.

My Visits to the Hospital

Vienna, July–August 1949

To my surprise, the tall, thin doctor directs his words to me: "*Fräulein*, we have a problem. Mr. Stein refuses to eat. He closes his lips tight when the sisters attempt to feed him. This is very serious. One sister found out that he will eat only if Elli feeds him."

Now I understand why the doctor is talking directly to me. "You must be Elli. He speaks your name often. *Fräulein*, can you come to feed him?"

"Yes, I can come."

"But there is a little problem. Mr. Stein wants you to prepare the food. He will eat only the food that you cook. Is that a possibility? Can you bring the cooked food here, every noon?"

"I don't know how to cook. But my mother will do it, I'm sure. And I can bring it here. I can feed him. No problem."

Mommy instantly agrees to do the cooking. On a small hot plate we received from a former neighbor, she makes potato, bean, or pea soup, pastas, and omelettes. I balance the pots and pans so as not to spill the food on the bumpy ride in the streetcar. The most difficult task is spoon-feeding Andy.

On the days when he receives treatment, his eyes do not focus, and he cannot open and close his mouth properly, so the food drips down the side of his face. It's painfully embarrassing. I must be more careful, concentrate better, I say to myself. In time, I learn to feed him without a mishap. On the days when he does not receive treatment, Andy eats with obvious appetite, able to swallow without a mess.

The treatments have a dramatic effect. They are electric shocks, administered directly to the brain. Daily I watch him get better and better. His eyes become more focused, and he starts to speak clearly. His hair begins to grow.

"Each shock is a minor death," Andy describes the treatment as his intellectual powers return. "I find it quite unbearable . . . the thought of dying . . . voluntarily. Each time . . . in my mind I compose a last testament, I instruct my eyes to soak up the sights of this world, for the last time." Andy speaks clearly, like a robot, in succinct, monotonous phrases.

"I detest the operating room . . . lying flat on my back . . . hands strapped to my side . . . the ritual of death," he intones. "The convulsions . . . the sensation of strangling . . . it lasts an eternity."

"I close my eyes," the singsong recitation goes on, "and make believe . . . I'm in the gas chamber . . . together with my parents . . . my mother . . . my father . . . little Anika . . . suffocating . . . suffocating . . . slowly." Andy's eyes are riveted on mine as he speaks, and I shudder. "Now I . . . I know . . . how they died."

Each day after we finish lunch, Andy repeats his incantation about the shock treatments. At first this is his only means of communication. With the passage of time, Andy becomes clinical in his description, less robotlike, and even able to evaluate the results.

My visits to the hospital become routine. Andy is allotted more and more freedom of movement. Eventually he waits for me near the entrance, and his face lights up like a bulb when he sees me. He is no longer in the triple-locked ward for the dangerously insane. He is in an open ward now—no locks, no attendants. I no longer have to feed him, but he still insists on eating only the food I bring him. We sit at a table until he finishes his lunch, then take long strolls in the yard, or sit under the ancient oak trees in the far corner of the garden.

During these beautiful summer afternoons I get to know Andy as I have never known him before. He is relaxed, and his discourse is less intense, less angry, more introspective. He displays a delightful sense of humor, even a sense of fun. We laugh at his quips, and my heart leaps with joy. He tells tales of his childhood without pathos or bitterness. I grow to like him. I like his proud bearing, his aristocratic features, his dark, wavy hair. Most of all, I like his magnificent dark eyes, which sparkle with obvious delight as he looks at me. And make me blush.

I must admit, I now look forward to the daily visits. Instead of trepidation, I approach the wrought-iron gates with suppressed excitement. Is it because of my share in Andy's dramatic improvement? Or is it something else?

I wonder: Would I reject his marriage proposal now? Although he admits that he asked the boys to stay away during my visits, he never makes reference to that fateful afternoon.

Is it because the memory is still too painful? I wish he would bring it up. It would give me a second chance to explain, to heal the hurt I inflicted.

My share in nursing him to health has created a bond between us. I believe Andy's attachment for me has deepened during these six weeks, and I am profoundly moved. I find myself thinking of him with great tenderness. Is this love?

On Sundays when all of us go to the hospital together, it's like old times. All the fun we used to have on our outings is now telescoped in the hospital visit. We have picnics in the hospital garden, play games, and laugh at impromptu jokes, giving free vent to our newfound optimism. The dramatic improvement in Andy's condition has released massive tensions.

Andy himself, although he is the reason for

our good humor, barely joins in the frolicking. He is not the same Andy with the everbrightening humor I meet every day when there are only the two of us. In the company of his closest comrades he is reserved and taciturn; he seems an outsider.

I am concerned by this change in Andy's mood. Is it due to his possessive feelings toward me? I am concerned and flattered at the same time.

I cannot discuss my concern with Mommy. She had warned me "not to encourage Andy's advances," and I am sure now she would advise me to stop seeing him. How could I listen to Mommy? How could I turn my back on Andy when he needs me?

I turn to Peter for help. From our first meeting in Bratislava I felt there was a special kinship between us, and I believe, if not for Andy's intense advances early on, Peter and I would have evolved a closer relationship. Although I do not disclose my inner turmoil, Peter senses my dilemma.

Evenings we go on long walks or sit in the park while Peter listens with great empathy and offers his unconditional support. Like a substitute brother, Peter's understanding and support restores my equilibrium and helps sort out my feelings.

After a while our talks shift away from Andy to other matters. There is so much to talk about. In Israel the course of events continues to ebb and flow. Although the fighting seems to have quieted somewhat, the war with the Arab nations is not over. There is a cease-fire, but no true peace. Friends who left on previous transports are in the army. The threat of a full-scale renewal of hostilities hangs above us as if we lived in Tel Aviv, Jerusalem, or Haifa.

Peter is not a fervent idealist like Andy, and therefore he is a better listener. He's more tolerant of differences of opinion. Peter and I talk, while Andy and I carried on ideological debates.

It is easier to relax in Peter's company. Peter observes and pokes fun, sometimes with refreshing wit, at other times with clever sarcasm. I enjoy the vastly different world according to Peter. It is a pragmatic world of the here and now, devoid of analyses. It is delightful, this lack of probing into painful areas of the psyche, and of the agonies of our past. A touch of Peter's cynicism, tidbits of gossip, mild ridicule of mutual friends—I find my summer evenings in Peter's company delightful.

Later in the summer Peter reveals that he has begun pondering the possibility of emigrating to America. He has contacted his relatives in New York for an affidavit.

"Peter, why have you decided to go to America?" I ask, stunned. "I thought you always wanted to go to Israel. I remember you telling me ages ago, in Bratislava, that you had made up your mind to go to Palestine, and now that it is our country, Israel, nothing can stop you from going there. What made you change your mind?"

Peter does not reply. My question seems to cause him discomfort. His face is like a beetroot when he finally answers: "Things changed . . . since then."

"What do you mean? How did things change? Has it become easier to get to America, to get a job in America? What about your plans to open a furniture plant in Israel? You expected a profitable future in furniture manufacturing, with the enormous influx of immigrants. Have you changed your mind about becoming a furniture tycoon?"

"No. Not really."

"Then what happened? As far as I can see, things have changed for the better in Israel. It is a Jewish State. The British are out for good. The road is open. The threat of Cyprus doesn't exist. Even the war with the Arabs has cooled somewhat."

All of a sudden, I remember Alex. Is Peter's change of plans related to Little Alex's fate? Now I think I understand Peter's reluctance to explain.

Little Alex was the gang's favorite. He was not the smallest in stature—on the contrary, Alex was rather tall. The appellation "Little" had to do with the fact that he was the youngest member, and they all doted on him. I do not remember meeting Alex, although the boys insist he was one of my charges and that I ran a number of errands for him in Bratislava. Alex left for Israel before I arrived in Vienna. Shortly after the gang reached the Rothschild Hospital, there was a transport, and Alex promptly signed up. The others opted for a brief rest in the American Zone before embarking on the arduous journey. Little Alex refused to "tarry in the Diaspora" and wait for his comrades. He could not be dissuaded from trying to reach the Land of Israel with the first opportunity that presented itself.

I do not remember meeting Alex, but I know him. He is with us at every outing, at every party, at every opera performance. His anecdotes are retold, his wit is emulated, and his best-known charades are reenacted. Little Alex's snapshots and almost daily letters have been copied and carried in the pocket of every gang member, to be passed around at a moment's notice. I have grown addicted to his personality almost as hopelessly as the others are.

About two weeks ago the letters stopped coming. And then bad news reached us. Little Alex is missing in action. During a "skirmish" he disappeared, and his body has not been found.

"There is faint hope," Little Alex's cousin wrote in a brief note from the army, "that Alex has been taken prisoner. It is, however, a bitter hope," the note concluded. "The Arabs torture and mutilate Jewish prisoners."

I am reluctant to ask Peter whether Little Alex's disappearance has had an impact on his change of plans. Peter is quiet as we walk back to our camp. We pause at the entrance to our room in awkward silence. Then Peter grips my arm with sudden fervor. "Elli, you don't understand me at all," he says with uncharacteristic passion.

I am taken aback, but when I search his face for an explanation, Peter averts his gaze and hurries toward the stairs. When he turns, his farewell is enigmatic, and his tone is sharper than usual: "Good night, Girl from Bratislava. See you tomorrow."

Mystified, I walk slowly to our room. What's the meaning of Peter's strange behavior? Why did he say that I don't understand him? Why did he call me "Girl from Bratislava" instead of Elli or "Little Sister"—the name all the gang members have adopted?

Mommy is not at home. Tommy is sitting at the school desk reading a letter from his sister Annie. Annie and her husband were unsuccessful in reaching Vienna at the beginning of

June but later managed to get to Italy, and from there to Israel.

Tommy has resumed his visits during Andy's stay in the hospital.

"It is kind of Tommy to keep you company in his brother's place," Mommy has observed. I believe Mommy is right. I welcome Tommy's friendship, especially since for some time Tommy had grown somewhat distant. I'm happy that for the sake of his brother Tommy has overcome his reserve. He has even begun buying little gifts, little tokens of thoughtfulness, just like his brother. I have told him how much I appreciate his kindness, but Tommy modestly dismisses my expressions of gratitude.

"You seem quiet," Tommy notes. "Something's the matter?"

I am thinking about Peter, trying to figure out his remarks. Luckily, without waiting for an answer, Tommy blurts out, "My sister Annie's pregnant. I'm going to be an uncle before the year's out."

"Great news, Tommy! Congratulations."

"Let me go tell Leslie and the others. They don't know yet. The letter has just arrived."

"A great homecoming present for Andy," I remind Tommy as he picks his way toward the exit.

Andy is being discharged from the hospital tomorrow. I am anticipating his return with great excitement. Once out of the hospital, I believe Andy will be more relaxed in the company of the gang, and things will be just as wonderful as before.

Good-bye, Vienna

Vienna, End of August 1949

"Where have you been?"

Mommy seems upset. "I've kept lunch waiting. You were out all afternoon, and no one knew where you were. You said you were going for a walk with one of the boys, but that was hours ago. What happened?"

"Mommy, the transport is leaving tomorrow!" I burst into tears. "All the boys are going."

Mother is flabbergasted. "Tomorrow? So soon?" She looks into my eyes, and I can see deep regret in her brilliant blue gaze. I know she likes the boys. But the regret is for my sake. "So they're leaving . . . I didn't expect it would happen so soon." Mommy arranges soup bowls, glasses, and cutlery on the narrow school desk that serves as our dining room table. "The food is getting cold," she says finally. "Let's eat."

We maneuver our bodies in between the

low desk and the narrow benches attached to it. Mommy ladles the soup into the bowls.

"Don't cry, Elli. Eat your soup," Mother says, and once again locks her penetrating blue stare into my soul. "What's the matter? If you want to go to Israel so badly, we'll talk about it. There will be other transports. We'll find a way."

"That's not it, Mommy." I swallow hard. "Something happened this afternoon." I must tell Mommy. I still taste it in my mouth. My stomach is churning.

How did it all happen?

Mommy was out, and I was reading Gandhi's autobiography, which someone lent me. I drew the blanket to shut out the neighborhood and enjoy the book in total privacy.

All at once I thought I recognized Andy's approaching footsteps, and I closed the book.

"May I come in?" It was Tommy's voice.

"Of course." I opened the blanket curtain. "Take a seat." But Tommy declined my offer. "Can we go for a walk?" he said with unexpected strain in his voice. "I must speak to you privately."

"Look. I can draw the curtain. It's perfect privacy."

Tommy shook his head. "I must talk to you. Not here. Can we go to the park?"

"Can it wait? Andy's supposed to come any minute."

"This is urgent. It won't take long."

I left word for Andy and Mommy with our neighbor Mr. Scheingold, who, as always, was deep in his correspondence. Tommy and I made our way between beds, chairs, desks, blankets, baby carriages, and bookcases out of the room, down the hallway, out of the building. I kept wondering, what's Tommy's urgency? Why doesn't he start speaking if it's so urgent?

In the park Tommy refused to take the first bench. Instead, we kept wandering through endless paths until, finally, Tommy found a sufficiently secluded spot. As soon as we sat down, Tommy leaned over and planted his lips on mine with such force that I was unable to breathe. His lips felt like wet steel clamps. Tommy's breath smelled of stale cigarette smoke, and I could feel my stomach churn. Finally, I managed to push his face away and extricate myself from his embrace. I started to run.

"Elli . . . Elli, please. Wait. I must speak to you. . . ."

With a few bounding strides Tommy caught up. "Elli, forgive me. Elli, I love you, I'm madly in love with you. Forgive me. I made a terrible mistake. Please, wait . . . can you forgive me? Can we talk?"

I paused, out of breath. "Okay. Talk. But . . . just talk."

"Please, let's sit down. I can't talk standing . . ."

"Sorry, you'll just have to. I'm not sitting down. I'm going back to camp. You can talk while we walk."

"Please, forgive me. I won't act crazy. Just . . . listen to me." Tommy sounded as if he was going to cry. I slowed down and leaned against a tree trunk. I could still taste his breath in my mouth and was fighting an urge to vomit. I took a deep breath.

"Okay. Speak. I'm listening."

For the next two hours Tommy held me prisoner of his anguished confessions. His voice trembling, he recounted the tale of his obsession with me, his abject misery as his twin brother preempted the "stage" and ordered him to keep his distance from his "fatal passion."

"The transport is leaving tomorrow. You must come with me and be my wife," Tommy shouted like a madman.

"Tomorrow? Since when have you known this?"

"I saw the notice as it was being posted and came to tell you immediately. The others don't know yet . . . Elli, if you don't marry me, I'll kill myself. I won't leave without you. Promise you'll come with me, or else I'll kill myself tonight."

"Tommy, for God's sake, don't say a thing like that!" Suddenly, I could not control my tears. Tommy also began to weep, and the two of us walked back to camp on paths covered with a carpet of fallen leaves. The summer was gone, and I felt my heart was going to break.

In the hallway we wiped each other's tears. Tommy climbed the stairs with slow, deliberate footsteps, and I approached our room, where Andy might be waiting. Instead, I found Mommy all agog with worry over my long absence.

"Eat your soup, Elli, while it's warm. You'll feel better," Mommy coaxes when I come to the end of my tale.

"Mommy, but what if he kills himself? I'll be responsible."

"Did you ask him how he'll do it?"

"Of course not. Oh, Mommy, what a question!"

"Don't worry, he won't kill himself." Mommy reassures me. "I hope you won't be offended if tomorrow you'll see him safe and sound, fully alive, aboard the transport van." I look at Mommy's amused face, the mischievous smile in her eyes, and despite my tears, I burst out laughing.

"Remember," Mommy warns, now smiling openly. "Next time a boyfriend threatens to kill himself, ask him how will he do it. It will kill his ardor."

I pray Mommy is right and Tommy will not do anything foolish tonight.

The next day the transport gathers in the hospital yard. One by one, my adopted brothers take their leave. Hayim presses his fountain pen into my palm. I had borrowed the precious writing tool, a rare item in the camp, several times. "It's yours," he whispers. "Write beautiful poems with it, and send me copies."

Stephan hands me a bouquet of lilies: "Your favorite." His handshake is firm. *"Hazak,"* he says in Hebrew. *"Hazak v'a-matz.* Be strong and of good courage."

"Hazak v'amatz," I mumble in response, and swallow hard.

Julius is holding his book of poetry in his hands. Is he going to read Ady, his Hungarian idol, on the truck across the Austrian and Italian hills, or aboard the refugee vessel to Haifa port? He hands me the book with an embarrassed smile. "I want you to keep this for me and bring it along when you come to Eretz Israel."

Peter and Andy—each has a parting gift, parting words. "As you see, it is Israel for me after all." Peter leans over and plants a kiss on my cheek and whispers, "You may not be aware, but I got my answer from you the other night. Without having to pop the question. I was luckier than Andy." Oh, God, Peter. How could I have known?

Andy puts his arms about me and gives me a brief, firm embrace. Then, for a fleeting moment, he places his cheek against mine. There are tears in his eyes, and I begin to weep.

Tommy is last. He averts his eyes as he shakes my hand. He turns abruptly and makes a run for the van.

"Tommy!" I shout, sobbing, but he does not turn back. With one leap he bounds up the rungs and vanishes into the van's interior.

Through a haze of tears I see the other boys wave before entering the covered army vehicle.

The convoy of vans moves out of the yard, and I stare into the cloud of exhaust fumes until the distant rumbling of the departing transport becomes a faint echo. I clutch the flowers and the other presents against my chest and move robotlike toward the hospital building.

The gang is gone, and I am to face Vienna without them. They are my friends, my brothers, my soul mates. How can I face life without them? Will I ever see them again?

I don't want to stay in Vienna any longer. We must find another way to get to America.

In our room I find an empty jar and put the lilies in water. They are my last reminder of the spring. The fabulous spring in Vienna that has just ended.

Tomorrow is September, and I must brace myself for the approaching winter. It is time to move on.

Back in Germany

Feldafing, September 1949

As the train approaches the German border, my stomach seems to be lodged in my throat. We are committing the most reprehensible act. We are returning to Germany.

"It won't be as bad as you think," Mommy reassures me. "Our friends will be happy to see us. We have no alternative. Might as well make the best of it." Mommy, the perennial pragmatist. For her, returning to Germany is just as unacceptable. Yet, she is able to extract an ounce of victory from every defeat.

She is right. We have attempted every other option. In Vienna we waited eight months for our turn on the Czechoslovak emigration list to the United States. The U.S. Congress has established an annual quota—a fixed number of emigrants allowed to enter the country each year. The number varies from country to country. The Czechoslovak quota is among the best, we were told by informed sources—among all nationalities the largest number of applications approved are from Czechoslovakia. When we applied for emigration at the U.S. Embassy in Prague over two years ago, we received a number and were told to expect our turn within two years.

"All you have to do," our sources advised, "is contact the U.S. Embassy in Vienna with your quota number and inform them that you recently left Prague for Vienna and wish to receive your American visa here."

In his letters Bubi approved of this course of action. I mustered my courage and, in the English I learned at the Folk Academy in Bratislava, presented our case to the officials at the U.S. Visa Section. It was the first time I spoke English to native speakers, and I was thrilled to discover they understood me. They took notes and told me, also in English, to come back in a few weeks for an answer. A few weeks later Mommy and I were admonished to wait for our turn patiently.

Finally, in September, we were informed by the Americans in Vienna that our Czechoslovak quota number could not be activated in Austria since Austria had its own quota. If we wanted to register on the Austrian quota, the Americans advised us, we had to establish Austrian residency. Once that was accomplished we could return to the U.S. Embassy and put our name on the Austrian emigration register. This response came as a painful blow. It was a transparent, disingenuous method of dismissal.

The Americans' rebuff was the last straw after the gang's departure. I no longer wanted to stay in Vienna. Mommy and I decided to follow friends' advice and register as refugees in a Displaced Persons Camp. Since the passage of the Refugee Emigration Act this year by the U.S. Congress, these D.P. Camps, holding Holocaust survivors and other refugees from all over Eastern Europe, offered the only hope of reaching America. It may be a matter of years, we were warned. Yet, it was an avenue. After the U.S. Embassy's crude delaying tactics in Vienna, to Mommy and me it seemed like the only avenue.

We packed our things once again and boarded a train for Linz. In the D.P. Camp near Linz there was no available room, so we went to Steyer, and then to Salzburg. These camps, too, overflowed with refugees and were unable to accommodate us.

There we were advised to proceed to Germany, where the D.P. Camps were still open to new arrivals. So Germany remained our last resort.

Night is descending rapidly as the train rushes through the Bavarian Alps. A shudder passes through my body. Once before I saw the terrible splendor of this countryside through the cracks of a cattle car carrying a human cargo of the wounded and dying.

"Are you cold?" Mommy pulls a sweater from my knapsack and drapes it about my shoulders. The train slows as it pulls into a station, and the conductor sings out the names of prospective stations. Munich is second on the chanted list.

"Munich! Did you hear the announcement?" Mommy springs into action. "We have to change trains there . . . for Feldafing. Let's get ready to disembark."

It is late at night when the train pulls into Feldafing. The stationmaster points to a cluster of dim lights hovering on top of the foothills, about a kilometer ahead. Those are the barracks of the D.P. Camp.

It is raining heavily, and we walk in deep, sticky mud on the road to the camp. Chill raindrops slam against our faces like sharp needles.

Vienna is far behind. The glorious spring, the radiant summer—were they only a dream?

Also far away is the sunny beach of Tel Aviv, the gently rolling hills of Jerusalem, and the azure blue water of the Kinneret. Far away is the Negev Desert, where the gang is doing army service now. The war is over; cease-fire agreements have been signed with most Arab nations. A melody of hope dances in the balmy air of the land. What am I doing here in the wet, cold, sticky German mud?

Our family relations—Ida, Gyuszi, Ily, and Jeno—welcome us warmly. "We have been waiting for you all week," Ily exclaims.

"All week? We've been awaiting your arrival ever since we got here," Ida adds. "Thank God you've finally arrived."

"From here at least there is some hope of getting to America," Jeno remarks, then adds a cautious qualifier: "Some hope. Some time in the future."

The four young people, nieces and nephews of my favorite Uncle Marton, spent a few weeks in Vienna, and there our family contact grew into friendship. When the four of them decided to continue their search for emigration opportunities in a D.P. Camp in Germany, they encouraged us to join them. Now we are here, and glad to see these congenial friends again. It is good to recapture fond memories and renew a sense of belonging. It is past midnight when we break for the night.

The camp consists of wooden bungalows built by the United Nations Relief and Rehabilitation Agency after the war to accommodate survivors who, instead of returning to their former countries, opted to remain in Germany—in transit to Palestine or the West.

"Tonight you'll sleep here in Ida and Gyuszi's bungalow," Jeno explains. "Tomorrow we'll find you a bungalow, or a room in a larger building, and take you to the camp's office to register. There you'll receive identity cards and food rations."

The two army cots set up for Mommy and me in Ida and Gyuszi's bungalow are a godsend. Within seconds after crawling under the coarse army blankets I sink into a deep sleep.

A short time later I am awakened by a relentless stream of cold rain hitting my blanket. There must be a hole in the ceiling right above me. Quietly I get out of bed and drag the cot away from under the column of pouring rain. But this is not sufficient. I must find some container to catch the water, otherwise the bungalow will be flooded by morning. I pad around barefoot on the soggy earthen floor in search of a vessel. I come upon a discarded oil can and place it under the leak. It proves to be a disastrous idea. The jet of water strikes the tin can with an incredible din, waking everyone in the bungalow. I toss the can outside. Gyuszi suggests draining the water from the bungalow. Shivering in the cold, wet night, we all join in digging narrow canals on the floor and a wide hole under the door to allow for drainage, and quickly return to our warm retreats under the blankets. But sleep eludes us; the incessant rivulet buffetting the mud floor keeps us awake all night.

At dawn, when light filters into the bungalow and I see my roommates sleeping peacefully at last, I feel better. Wading in a deep carpet of water, I get dressed, put on my raincoat and scarf, and succeed in tiptoeing out of the bungalow unnoticed.

I head for the train station. I must get to Munich to find a job. I need a pair of rubber boots, warm stockings, and gloves. And so does Mommy. Where will we get the money to buy these? There is only fifty dollars left from the proceeds of the house sale, and we are saving that for starting a life in America. If we ever get there!

A leaden curtain of rain obscures my first glimpses of Munich as I emerge from the train station. The terminal building is under repair, and I make my way among stacks of brick, wooden beams, and barrels of mortar out into the streets of the Bavarian capital.

The first policeman I come across knows that there is a synagogue and a rabbi in Munich. He also knows that I can obtain the rabbi's address from the police, and directs me to the nearest police station.

Against the onslaught of unrelenting rain,

I march toward Moehlstrasse, the new Jewish ghetto in Munich. Mostly East-European Jewish refugees congregate in Moehlstrasse, a once busy commercial street totally leveled by Allied bombing. Here, in makeshift wooden huts, Jews from Poland, Romania, and Hungary opened little shops, injecting vitality into a ghost district. The simple but colorful Jewish shops are the only signs of life in the entire area. Moehlstrasse's side streets are partial ruins: buildings with parts of the walls blown away; others with upper floors, or roofs missing.

I enter one of these buildings and knock gently on a narrow door with peeling brown paint. It is the address of Rabbi and Mrs. Herschel Blau. The door is opened by a youngish man of medium height with a trim brown beard.

"Can I help you?" the rabbi's dark brown eyes register astonishment. I realize the unexpected appearance of a young blond girl on his doorstep in the gray hours of the morning calls for an explanation.

"May I talk to you?"

The rabbi opens the door wider and, still hesitant, bids me to enter. "This way, please."

I follow the rabbi through a clean, neatly furnished living room into the kitchen. "It's warmer in here," he says in way of explanation. A young woman with a kerchief about her head turns from her cooking stove and stares at me in shock. The "rebbetsen," the rabbi's wife, is a pleasant-looking woman in her late twenties.

"I am a teacher of Hebrew and Jewish studies," I begin by way of introduction, and notice that both husband and wife seem even more astonished. "I wonder whether there's a Jewish school here. I'm looking for a job." The couple gaze at me in stunned silence. I continue, now somewhat uncertainly. "My mother and I arrived from Austria late last night. We are staying with friends in Camp Feldafing."

"Feldafing? You came in from Feldafing this morning? In this horrible weather! You must've left at dawn. Have you had breakfast?" Without waiting for an answer, the rebbetsen declares, "You need something to warm you up."

"Thank you," I reply, and for some strange, inexplicable reason, tears spring to my eyes. "A cup of coffee would be fine."

The rebbetsen helps me out of my raincoat

and hangs it near the stove to dry. She points to a large stool. "Sit here, *Fräulein*, this is a warm corner."

Within seconds there is a steaming bowl of oatmeal, buttered toast, and a mug of hot coffee in front of me on the kitchen table. During breakfast I find out that the rabbi and rebbetsen, recently married here in Munich, are themselves refugees from Eastern Europe, she from Poland, and he from Romania. I also find out there is no Jewish school in Munich, but the rabbi promises to investigate job opportunities for me. Both insist that I stay with them for the Sabbath. When I politely decline, explaining that Mommy is expecting my return, they seem sincerely disappointed and make me promise to bring Mommy along for a visit soon. The rebbetsen presses a loaf of homemade *kuchen* on me and helps me into my coat, dried in the warmth of her kitchen stove.

From the bombed-out building where the rabbi of Munich and his wife make their home, I carry away a secret spark. The grim first morning in Germany holds a ray of hope that propels me toward yet another new beginning.

Camp Feldafing

September 1949–October 1950

Villa Park used to be the summer home of a German family in the resort area of Feldafing, the playground of the country's wealthy elite. A whole string of these elegant villas, riding the hill above the barracks and bungalows of Camp Feldafing, is now part of the camp. Through Jeno's connections, Mommy and I receive a room in Villa Park.

Where are the former residents of these villas? Where are the pampered masters who used to occupy all twenty rooms of the villa, ride their horses on the lovely downs nearby, sail their boats on the lake at the bottom of the hill, or race their cars on the autobahn in the vicinity?

Rumor has it that the families of top Nazis expropriated these luxury residences from the original owners. After the Nazis fled from the approaching Allied forces, the abandoned villas came under the authority of the International Refugee Organization, the IRO, which allocated them for our use, each room to another family. A strange hierarchy—German aristocrats, Bavarian Nazis, Jewish refugees. Mommy and I are the latest beneficiaries of the unpredictable pecking order.

I need not have worried about a job. Two days after our arrival I meet a former pupil from my Beth Jacob class in Bratislava. Soon a group of parents approach me with a request: Would I organize a Beth Jacob school for girls in the camp? Within a week after the commencement of my Beth Jacob classes, Mrs. Furman, the camp public school principal, offers me a position as teacher of English. English language is a compulsory subject in the curriculum of this elementary school administered by the Jewish Agency and run by the Refugee Central Committee.

So now I am an English teacher on Monday, Wednesday, and Friday mornings, and a teacher of Jewish subjects after school. The public school job affords me a wonderful opportunity to learn both Hebrew and English. As the language of instruction in the elementary school is exclusively Hebrew, I am required to teach English through the medium of Hebrew. Since I am proficient neither in English nor in Hebrew, I study late into the night, sometimes until dawn, in preparation for each class.

Even with all this feverish preparation I find myself only one step ahead of my classes. As if they feel my enthusiasm for the challenge of teaching, the children seem to relish learning English. They are eager to learn new words and often help me find the corresponding Hebrew words.

The children in my classes speak many languages. Although Yiddish is the official language of the camp, the children chat in Polish, Romanian, Russian, and Hungarian among themselves. The school, however, is a microcosm of modern Israel—here the language is exclusively Hebrew. My pupils carry me along on the adventure of learning all about the country while learning the language. It's thrilling to grow together with my pupils.

Two or three weeks later I get a job teaching English in Munich at the ORT Vocational

School and at the Hebrew Gymnasium on Tuesdays and Thursdays. I love to take the train to Munich in the mornings and conduct classes to my peers at the gymnasium, and in the afternoons to people many years my senior at the ORT.

Just when I think my every free moment is occupied, Rabbi Blau introduces me to a Habad group, an intellectual branch of the Hasidic movement, and I am assigned the most exciting task of my teaching career. I become part of an outreach project—on Sundays I travel with a team of Hasidic scholars to conduct lectures on Judaism at the various D.P. Camps throughout the American Zone in Germany. I get to know many places and meet many people. I get to know and touch many lives.

Soon after our arrival in the D.P. Camp, Mommy and I register for emigration under the U.S. Refugee Act and begin the wait for our turn on the refugee list.

While we wait, fall turns into frosty winter, then bright spring, and then the shimmering heat of summer is exchanged, once again, by heavy autumn rains. A year passes, and we are still waiting. And while we wait, we become old-timers in the D.P. Camp.

Mommy is sewing again, this time by hand. We have no sewing machine, but this handicap does not daunt her. Neither does the partial paralysis of her hand, the result of an injury to her spine in Auschwitz. With the support of an elastic bandage wrapped tightly around her wrist, Mommy practices moving her fingers nimbly, and learns to stitch with amazing speed. While making beautiful dresses for little girls, Mommy makes many close friends among their mothers.

Bubi is a senior at Yeshiva University in New York. He has a Kodak camera and is fond of taking pictures. In every letter we find marvelous snapshots of himself, his friends, Uncle Abish and his family, and of the university campus. I can barely recognize Bubi in these pictures. God, how he has changed since we parted three and a half years ago.

"I hope and pray," he writes, "that you will be here for my graduation."

Despite my intense involvement in multifarious activities, I carry with me a nagging sense of void, a raw yearning to be near him again. Next July my brother will graduate from college. Please God, let me be there.

Good news reaches us from Israel. My friend Ellike, happily married to her cousin Moshe, is going to be a mother. Many of the other girls from the Home are also married and are busy building new lives.

The gang members have all been released from the military. They are no longer a group—the realities of life have scattered them to distant parts of Israel. Andy found employment as a male nurse in a Jerusalem hospital. Tommy joined a *kibbutz* on the Syrian border in the north. Leslie, now a married man, retrained as an electrician and works for the Herzlia municipality. Peter is pursuing his ambition as an apprentice in a Tel Aviv furniture plant. Hayim waits on tables in a Beersheba restaurant. Julius and Stephan work at Tel Aviv University—Julius the poet in the library, and studious Stephan, attending classes by day and cleaning corridors by night.

By the end of the year, emigration to Israel is moving apace. As the number of residents dwindles and the number of vacant bungalows grows, the camp starts to resemble a ghost town. Rumors begin to circulate that Camp Feldafing will be liquidated. Where will they move us?

The rumors materialize sooner than we expect. Even before the first snowfall, we, the small remnant of the once abundant camp, are transferred to Camp Geretsried, a small encampment in the heart of a pine forest near the Bavarian village of the same name.

Camp Feldafing is a thing of the past.

Camp Geretsried

October 1950–February 1951

The van drives through spectacular mountain passes on its approach to Geretsried and it pulls up at the gate of a dense pine forest. The gate opens, and the van rolls into a clearing at the center of the wood. Only moments later do bungalows become partially visible among the trees.

"What do you know! This must be our camp."

Mommy's enthusiasm is quickly ignited. "Children, I believe Elli is right. This must be the camp. Look at the bungalows hidden under the trees."

For Mommy, Jeno, Ily, Ida, and Gyuszi, all in their twenties, are like her children. They have been anticipating the move from Feldafing with trepidation, and the inexplicable journey into a forest has not allayed their anxiety. But now their spirits begin to rise.

This place is enchanting. It looks like a scenic summer camping site.

My knowledge of German, Yiddish, Hungarian, Slovak, a smattering of Russian, and my typing skill land me a job in the office of the camp administration. Slovak is especially helpful as a key to a number of Slavic languages. In a short time I serve as the emigration officer, filling out applications for those who register for emigration. Through my job I come in contact with every resident of Camp Geretsried, and our circle of friends becomes enormous. Mommy once again turns her sewing skills to dressmaking, and our bungalow turns into a popular meeting place.

A new, painful reality confronts us during the winter. All at once the emigration of refugees to the U.S.A. slows to a trickle. The anti-Communist campaign of Senator Joseph McCarthy influences American policy. Everyone from "behind the Iron Curtain" has become suspect, and the number of those allowed to enter the country is drastically reduced. We are hurt and confused—we cannot understand why the Americans have attached the stigma of Communism to us. No one in America, not even Senator McCarthy, detests Communism as much as the refugees who have escaped from the fangs of Communist regimes. Why don't the Americans realize this?

One day, unexpectedly, a U.S. military commission called the Criminal Investigation Division (CID) arrives to investigate every refugee who registered for the U.S.A. Because of the commission's unconcealed bias, the majority of the applications end up stamped with UNFIT FOR U.S. EMIGRATION. As emigration officer, it is my unwelcome duty to notify the applicants.

The CID becomes a permanent fixture. Every week two CID officers arrive to interrogate each applicant, and I serve as interpreter. During the interviews two CID officers sit facing the applicant and his family and shoot a barrage of questions at them in rapid English. I have to be extremely careful to make sure I understand the questions perfectly and translate them correctly. A mistake may prove very grave for the applicant's future. The questions take us by surprise with their accusatory tone and content:

"Why do you want to go to America?"

"Were you a member of the Communist Party?"

"Were you a member of a subversive organization?"

"No? Where is your proof?"

"Where are your documents?"

"Where were you from 1946 to 1950?"

"Where is your proof? Where are your documents to prove that you did not live in a Communist country in those years?"

"You escaped from Poland? Where is your proof?"

"You escaped from Czechoslovakia? Where is your proof?"

"You escaped from Hungary? Where is your proof?"

"Why don't you have proof? Perhaps you are lying. We can't take your word alone for it. We need written proof."

"Witnesses? What good are witnesses? Why should we trust your witnesses? We need written proof. Written proof. Only written proof."

Do the Americans not understand the catastrophic conditions that forced tens of thousands to flee for their lives, without documents, without recorded words? Are the Americans unaware of these realities?

I translate the answers and explanations, the pleas. The refugees who have no written evidence to substantiate their accounts, their life stories, are turned away from the shores of America, the land of their dreams.

The story of David, one of my pupils at the ORT School, is a heart-wrenching example of the many tragedies. After the war David found out that his brother was alive in Denver, Colorado. Although he dreamed of going to Palestine, David registered for emigration to America in the summer of 1946. Sadly, he watched his closest friends leave for the Jewish land, but because his yearning to be reunited with his brother in America was more compelling, David stayed in the D.P. Camp, waiting patiently for his turn.

Now it is the early winter of 1951, and finally David's turn has come. This time I am not concerned about the CID officer's stern questioning. David has an ID card from the International Refugee Organization (IRO), dated 1946, stating that he has been a resident of the D. P. Camp since then. David is the rare refugee who has written proof that he never lived behind the Iron Curtain. He is guaranteed clear sailing.

"Will you be a loyal citizen of the United States?" the CID officer inquires after the standard questions have been answered satisfactorily.

"Of course I will be a loyal citizen," David says in Yiddish, and I translate.

"If drafted, will you join the armed forces of the United States? In case of war, are you ready to fight for the United States of America?"

"Yes. As a United States citizen, it's only natural that I—"

"I have another question," the American officer interrupts. "Suppose the United States of America goes to war with Israel and you as a United States citizen are drafted into the army. Will you unhesitatingly bear arms against Israel? Will you unhesitatingly shoot at Israeli soldiers?"

My voice trembles as I translate. David turns as white as a ghost. I want to whisper, "Say yes." But I know he wouldn't. I know

David. He won't lie even though his future depends on it. As I have expected, David is silent.

"I demand an answer. Are you prepared to fight for your country the United States against Israel?"

David raises his eyes and looks straight into those of the American. "I will not shoot a fellow Jew."

My voice shakes as I translate.

The interview is over. The CID officer hands me David's application. Stamped across the face of the top sheet, in large red letters, are the words: UNFIT FOR U.S. EMIGRATION.

The next morning David's body is found dangling from the roof beam of his bungalow.

The names of the fortunate ones are posted in the hallway outside the offices of the IRO in Gauting. Jeno is in the habit of taking the train to Gauting every morning to check the list. From my office window I watch him return to the camp gate every noon. I can tell from his gait and the slump of his shoulders that his name is still missing from the list. As the day wears on his posture straightens, and by the evening he even jokes around among friends in our bungalow. Jeno's day consists of this cycle: Gauting, gloom, recovery.

One morning Jeno comes through the camp gate with an erect posture. He smiles mysteriously as he walks through the door of my office. I expect him to blurt out the good news. But Jeno tarries.

"So? Speak, for God's sake."

All at once, a cloud passes over his countenance. The smile is gone.

"Ida, Gyuszi, Ily, and myself. Our names are on the list. Aunt Laura and you . . . yours are not."

I swallow hard. "Jeno, congratulations. I'm happy for you."

We have become a family, the six of us, and I feel truly happy that they have made it. Especially Jeno. He has been deeply concerned about the CID investigations.

"Elli"—Jeno reaches for my hand and gives it a squeeze—"you'll see, you and Aunt Laura will come next. Very soon."

"I believe you. I believe it's a matter of days for us, too."

"You know what I think? I think your permit is delayed because they need you here.

Who would be able to take your place? Especially as interpreter. Who can translate from German, Hungarian, Slovak, and the other Slavic languages? I am convinced that's the reason."

"That's nonsense. But thanks, anyway, Jeno. Your good luck gives me new hope."

I watch with mixed emotions the four friends who have become brothers and sisters prepare for the big journey. I am saddened by the thought of their departure, yet caught up in the excitement of their momentous happening. Mommy and I go shopping in Munich for parting gifts—a fountain pen for each. In addition, Mommy sews a new dress for each of the two young women.

At the end of February, when crocuses appear on the brown patches in the snow, the four of them take their farewell.

Once again my life becomes an empty platform for departing trains. The sound of good-byes rings in my ears, lingers in my soul. My God, how much longer?

When will the day come when I will wave good-bye to the empty platform from the window of a departing train?

"So It Has Come to Pass . . ."

March 19–30, 1951

The emigration office is quiet these days. All transports to Israel are gone. Most camp residents who were registered for the United States have switched to other destinations—Canada, Cuba, South America—and their emigration permits have come through. They, too, are long gone. All our friends are gone.

A dismally cold, wet winter drags on and on. Is it merely a reflection of the winter in my soul? Passover is in four weeks. One more Passover in Germany. How many more Passovers? How many more years? Will we ever reach America?

Mommy and I were interrogated by the CID over two weeks ago. Why don't they let us know the results? Even a dismissal would be easier to bear than this maddening uncertainty.

I must be having Monday blues. It is indeed a bleak Monday morning. I have a sinking feeling of abandonment. I miss the friends with whom I shared so much of my daily trials and joys. They have all gone to distant parts. Hershu, Laci, Irene, Bronia, Arnold; the Ganzfried, Braun, Grunstein, and Markusz families—where are they now? Ily, Sanyi, Ida, and Gyuszi are fond, aching memories. Jeno's absence is a gaping wound.

The picture postcard I received from Jeno is propped up on my typewriter. As I glance at it, I cannot conceive of ever spanning the distance between us. From my window I can survey the deserted square of the camp and the surrounding bungalows, all vacant. Someone just entered the gate and is approaching across the square. It's Otto, who always hangs around the office, eager for small talk. He is always bright-eyed and bushy-tailed in the morning. I'm not ready to cope with good cheer and small talk this morning. I hope he is not on his way here.

There is a knock on the door, and Otto enters, his face aglow. "Good morning, Elli. I have good news for you."

"Really?" I ask, annoyed. "What is your good news this morning?"

"Wouldn't you like to know?" Now Otto pokes his smiling face between me and the typewriter, ostentatiously concealing a sheet of paper behind his back. The last thing I need this morning is teasing from a fellow I wish hadn't dropped in.

"Okay, Otto. Pray tell."

Otto annoyingly waves the paper before my eyes. "Here it is! The emigration list, with the names Elli Friedmann and Laura Friedmann right on top. You are instructed to leave immediately for the transit camp in Munich."

"What?! Let me see that paper. Otto, let me see the paper!"

Otto ceremoniously spreads the sheet on the desk, and there are our names, right on top of twenty or thirty others who received permits to emigrate to the United States.

"How did you get this?"

"I went to Gauting this morning, to check the list. And there it was!"

"But you are not going to America. Why did you go to Gauting?"

"I went for you. I wanted to be the one to tell you if there was good news."

"Otto, you're an angel!" I wrap my arms

about his long neck. "Thank you. Thank you." Otto's happiness matches my own. He takes my hands into his, and we begin to dance the *hora*. "*Hevenu Shalom aleichem . . .*" We bring you peace.

"Otto, would you mind the office for a few minutes? I must run and tell Mommy. Oh, God, how wonderful!"

Without waiting for Otto's answer I dash off toward our bungalow. Mommy's eyes open wide with surprise when I show her the list. "So it has come to pass . . . finally!" I lock her in my arms. "Mommy. Yes. Yes. Yes. It has come to pass. At last. At long last." I hold her tight in my arms. "Can you believe it, Mommy? It's come to pass!"

Then I remember. "Oh, Mommy, we have to start packing immediately. On Thursday morning we have to report to the Funk Kaserne, the transit camp in Munich. We have to be packed by then."

"Okay. I'll start right away."

I plant a kiss on Mommy's cheek and gallop back to the office.

"Gauting has just called," Otto announces proudly. "To notify you of the permit and tell you to be ready for a Thursday morning departure. I did not tell them you already knew," he adds, justifiably pleased with himself.

In a year and a half the volume of our belongings has increased considerably, but Mommy manages to fit everything into two suitcases. The night before our departure turns into a string of leave-taking from neighbors and even casual acquaintances. Why is it still so painful? We are not leaving close friends behind. And yet . . . every parting is a minor death.

We are lucky. Our stay at the transit camp in Munich lasts only three days. On Sunday morning the transport van begins the journey toward Bremerhaven, the northern German port from which the refugee ships sail for America.

Then we are quartered at the U.S. military compound near Bremerhaven for an indefinite waiting period. Every morning rumors leap from barrack to barrack like wildfire.

"The boat is here! The boat is in the harbor. We are leaving today!"

Later in the day the rumor changes to: "The boat is here, but we're not leaving today.

We are leaving tomorrow morning."

Somewhat later the rumor is totally revised: "The boat in the harbor is not for us. It is for transport of U.S. military personnel. No one knows when our boat will arrive." And despair sets in.

Rumor mongers spread hope, doubt, disappointment, and uncertainty as a daily diet. The constant apprehension is debilitating. Will our ship ever sail?

Finally, on Thursday an official announcement is made. We are to set sail on Saturday afternoon. Boarding the ship will commence early Saturday morning.

Excitement ripples through the ranks of the refugees.

Mommy and I, however, receive the announcement with alarm. Jewish law, called *halakhah,* prohibits travel on the Sabbath. In the case of an ocean voyage, one is permitted to spend the Sabbath aboard a ship that has sailed before the commencement of the Sabbath. But boarding a ship on the Sabbath is forbidden.

What should we do? Our strict observance of Jewish law dictates that we wait for the next sailing. Will the authorities allow us to stay here until the next refugee boat? When will that be? Perhaps we will be stranded here until after Passover. How can we properly observe the dietary laws of Passover in this camp without cooking facilities?

Mommy and I spend the night agonizing over the terrible dilemma. Before dawn, an idea fills me with ecstasy. "Mommy, I've found a solution! According to *halakhah*, we are permitted to sail on the Sabbath provided we board the ship the day before. I am going to volunteer for work on the ship as interpreter, or anything else, and request permission for the two of us to board on Friday."

"It sounds like a wonderful idea," Mommy responds thoughtfully. "But . . . will they go along?"

"I'm sure. I'll explain our problem, and I'm sure they'll cooperate."

I am lucky to find Mr. Nemec, the IRO representative, in his office early in the morning. He listens to my offer with interest. "It's up to the Americans. I'll put you in touch with Captain McGregor. He's in charge of assignments."

After a few brief words Mr. Nemec replaces the receiver: "He wants to see you at once. Do you know how to get to Captain McGregor's staff room?" Then, instead of giving me directions, he rises from his desk. "You know what?" he says cheerfully. "I'll take you over there. Come." Mr. Nemec leads me to an army jeep behind the barrack and holds the door open on the passenger's side.

I remember a ride in another jeep, to the Haganah camp in the Moravian hills. How long ago was that? My God, how very long ago.

Captain McGregor is pleased with my offer. "Your English is great!" the tall man in a trim uniform exclaims with enthusiasm. "Fine. Great. You'll be my interpreter. God only knows I need an interpreter. Even for my own crew I need an interpreter! So it's settled. You come see me tomorrow morning, bright and early, and I'll give you your assignment."

"But . . . there's something else. You see, my mother and I, we would like to board the ship today. Perhaps you can give me my assignment today."

"Today? But why?"

"You see, my mother and I, we are Jewish,

and it's forbidden for us to sail on the Sabbath . . . that is, to board the ship on the Sabbath. As long as we board the ship before the commencement of the Sabbath, like on Friday, it's okay. I know it's hard to understand."

"I understand. No problem. The crew is boarding today. You and your mother can board together with the crew. That's fine with me. Bring your things to my office, and I'll take you aboard. Then we can start working together right away. It's a fine idea!"

"Thank you, Captain. You're an angel."

"Don't let my crew hear that!" Captain McGregor explodes. The furrows on his dark-complexioned face multiply as his melodious chuckle swells into a boisterous belly laugh. "An angel? Not bad. Not bad!"

Captain McGregor's laughter surprises me. At first glance I thought he had a rather ascetic appearance, but now I notice how his eyes sparkle. I'm glad. The journey across the ocean is to take eight days. I prefer to spend it in the company of a man with a mischievous twinkle in his eyes.

Mommy is overjoyed. "Wonderful!" She

embraces me, rubbing her cheek against mine. "So you did it, my daughter. You did it, again."

Mommy's praise unexpectedly brings tears to my eyes. Does she really believe I have become a competent adult?

Still laughing with relief, Mommy picks up the larger suitcase. "I'm ready. Let's go to America! Show me the way to this captain's office."

With a suitcase in one hand and a small package of food in the other, I lead the way across the open square. Captain McGregor meets us near the flagpole. He shakes hands with Mommy and hands our luggage to a U.S. Marine. Then he directs us to board one of the U.S. Navy trucks lined up on the far end of the spacious quadrangle.

"Those trucks will take you to the ship. Johnnie here will show you to your quarters. I'll see you aboard the *General Stewart*." Captain McGregor gives us a smart salute, and we head toward the military vehicles.

Mommy and I cross the square, past the flagpole flying the American flag. It is so simple. You walk to the trucks that will take you to the ship going to America. You simply walk away from Germany. From Europe. From this cursed continent and its blood-soaked earth. Its mass graves.

There is no good-bye. There is only hello. To the ocean and its timeless, infinite majesty, which separates you from the anguished past. To the distant horizon.

To America, and the hope of a better future.

Epilogue

On April 7, 1951, on a sunny Sabbath morning, our boat, the *General Stewart*, docked in New York Harbor. My brother Bubi was waiting on the pier, his radiant face rising above the crowd. In our long, tearful embrace, four years of anguish melted. I knew I had arrived to a safe haven.

My uncle Abish and his wife, Aunt Lilli, were also there to greet us. The five of us walked out of the harbor, heading for their apartment in the vicinity. It was an hour's walk on the homely, sun-splashed streets of New York's Lower East Side—my first encounter with America.

In the years that followed, America was kind to me. During the first year I became both a teacher and a student. By passing exams for a Hebrew teacher's diploma I qualified for teaching, and by passing a high school equivalency test I qualified for entering college. In time I moved from first grade to teaching higher grades, then high school, and eventually I became a college professor, learning all along from my students of all ages.

Teaching by day and attending college in the evening, it took ten years to complete my studies for a B.A. degree. By then I was married and the mother of two children. My little boy graduated from kindergarten, my little girl from diapers, and I from college all on the same day.

While my children grew I continued teaching and studying, in time earning a master's degree and then a Ph.D. I also kept writing. In addition to the theses, I wrote articles, poetry, and the beginning of my first memoir. My children claim that the only lullaby they ever heard was the clicking sound of my typewriter, and whenever they reached for a snack into the refrigerator, all they fished out of the fruit bin were stacks of paper. (I had the habit of storing my manuscripts in the refrigerator for safekeeping against fire.) I am sure both claims are slightly exaggerated, and yet on reflection I can't help but believe that my thirst for learning and urge to record all I have learned and remembered must have been taxing on my family.

My mother was our next-door neighbor and derived great joy from the company of her grandchildren, including the growing family of my brother Bubi, who came on frequent visits from his suburban Long Beach, where he served as principal of a Hebrew day school. My mother and I *did* attend his graduation and later his rabbinical ordination from Yeshiva University.

On a brilliant day in July 1977, twenty-six years after we reached New York Harbor, Mommy and I landed at Ben Gurion Airport in Tel Aviv as new immigrants in Israel. By then my mother was in her eighties, my son was married, and my daughter was a freshman in college. I was facing a new marriage, and motherhood to my future husband's teenage son and daughter.

During the twenty-two years that passed since that day, I continued conducting classes at my college, commuting between my new home in Israel and my old home in New York. This afforded me an opportunity to interrelate with my students and share in the lives of my children in America and my stepchildren in Israel, who in the interim have achieved successes as professionals and as dedicated parents. Participating in the lives of my grandchildren—their interests, talents, achievements, friendships, and aspirations—is a new, exciting chapter of my life. My brother and his wife recently sold their home in Long Beach, New York, where they lived for forty years, and moved to Jerusalem, the capital of Israel, to live near their children and their growing families.

The decade Mommy spent in Israel were the happiest years of her life. Many years ago my husband and I had the privilege of fulfilling my mother's last request and bringing the remains of her parents from Europe to be buried in Israel. A dam was being built on the Danube near the abandoned Jewish cemetery in Czechoslovakia, and my grandparents' graves would have been submerged under the river.

Ten years ago, at the age of ninety-three, my mother died and found eternal rest in Jerusalem next to her beloved parents. The triple tomb has become a family shrine that, unlike every other trace of our past destroyed by the Holocaust, will remain a monument to our roots.

God blessed our long search with a home in Israel, where my family now has a permanent landmark for future generations.

Appendix A

Our Family After the Holocaust:
Chronicle of Events

JUNE 1945 We return to Šamorín after
liberation.

JULY 1945 We receive news of my father's
death.

SEPTEMBER 1945 I am back in school.

NOVEMBER 1945 A stranger returns
Daddy's coat.

DECEMBER 1945 I find out about *Briha*
from Miki.

SPRING 1946 Miki and Barishna leave for
Palestine.

JULY 1, 1946 I leave with the boys' and
girls' camps for the Tatras.

JULY 7, 1946 Frieda leaves the Tatras. I am
left alone in charge of the girls' camp.

AUGUST 11, 1946 The children and I escape

from the partisans in the Tatras.

SEPTEMBER 1946 I enroll at the teachers'
seminary in Bratislava.

MARCH 20, 1947 My brother leaves for
America.

NOVEMBER 29, 1947 The UN votes to
partition Palestine and establish a Jewish
State; Zionist youths dance in the Square.

DECEMBER 1947–MARCH 1949 My
involvement in work for the *Briha*.

FEBRUARY 1948 The Communists take over
the government of Czechoslovakia.

MARCH 1948 My attempt to enroll in the
Haganah camp is rejected; I am appointed
school headmistress.

SEPTEMBER 10–22, 1948 My work in road
construction above the Danube; I meet Vilo.

MARCH 8, 1949 Mommy and I are crossing
the border to Vienna.

SEPTEMBER 1949 We leave Vienna.

SEPTEMBER 1949–OCTOBER 1950 Mommy

and I are residents of Camp Feldafing.

OCTOBER 1950–FEBRUARY 1951 Mommy
and I are residents of Camp Geretsried.

MARCH 19–30, 1951 Our last days in
Germany.

APRIL 7, 1951 We arrive in New York.

Appendix B

Post-Holocaust Period:
Highlights of Chronology

MAY 7, 1945 Germany surrenders. The war ends in Europe.

SUMMER 1945 Displaced Persons Camps established in American and British Zones of Germany and Austria. President Harry Truman sends emissary, Earl Harrison, to visit D.P.s. His recommendation: 100,000 Jewish survivors be sent to Palestine immediately.

FEBRUARY 1946 Anglo-American Committee of Inquiry recommends that a binational Jewish-Arab government be set up in Palestine.

NOVEMBER 1945–OCTOBER 1946 War crimes trials are held in Nuremberg, Germany.

APRIL 1947 General Assembly of the UN sets up eleven-nation board, the UN Special Committee on Palestine (UNSCOP), to deal with the Palestine impasse.

NOVEMBER 29, 1947 General Assembly of the UN votes to partition Palestine and establish sovereign Jewish and Arab states; beginning of widespread Arab attacks.

FEBRUARY 1948 Communists take over the government of Czechoslovakia.

MAY 14, 1948 Ben-Gurion reads the Declaration of Independence of Israel; seven Arab armies invade the infant state; Israel wages war of independence.

1949 First Knesset opens; Chaim Weizmann becomes the first president of Israel; David Ben-Gurion elected the first prime minister; cease-fire agreements with Egypt, Lebanon, Transjordan, Syria; Israel becomes a member of the UN; 240,000 immigrants enter the country.

1951 Second Knesset is elected; tension on borders increases; mass immigration continues.

Glossary of Terms

Affidavit—a-fah-DAY-vit—a voluntary, sworn declaration in writing—LATIN

Briha—BRI-ha—flight, or escape—HEBREW

Bunker—BUN-ker—underground barrack—OLD SWEDISH

Burg—BOORG—castle—GERMAN

CARE (Cooperative American Remittances Everywhere) —nonprofit organization begun after World War II to send food and clothing overseas

Diaspora—die-AS-pa-ra—the dispersion of the Jews outside their homeland—GREEK

Eretz—EH-retz—land—HEBREW

Fräulein—FROY-line—Miss—GERMAN

Ghetto—GE-toh—a part of a city or town where Jews were forced to live—ITALIAN

Gymnasium—jim-NAE-zee-um—classical secondary school—LATIN

Haganah—ha-ga-NAH—defense, voluntary fighting units, later to become the Israel Defense Forces—HEBREW

Halakhah—ha-LAH-kha—Jewish law—HEBREW

Hanukkah—HAH-noo-kah—Jewish holiday (usually in December) celebrating the successful revolt against Greco-Syrian occupation and liberation of Judea from religious oppression—HEBREW

Havera—ha-VEH-rah—friend (*f*)—HEBREW

Kibbutz—ki-BUHTS—collective settlement, commune—HEBREW

Kuchen—KOO-khin—a yeast-dough coffee cake—GERMAN

Maccabees—MA-kuh-beez—Jewish patriots who led a successful revolt against the overwhelming might of the Greco-Syrian empire—HEBREW

Mizrachi—miz-RAH-khi—religious Zionist organization—HEBREW

Nazdar—NAH-zdahr—greeting—CZECH and SLOVAK

Nie nada—NEE NAH-duh—"Nothing doing"—RUSSIAN

ORT (Organization for Rehabilitation and Training)—network of vocational schools

Pan—PAHN—Mr.— CZECH and SLOVAK

Pharaohs—FAR-ohz—ancient Egyptian monarchs who enslaved the Jews—EGYPTIAN

Prater—PRAH-ter—famous Viennese amusement park

Raison d'être—rae-ZONE de-TRE—reason for being, rationale for existing—FRENCH

Riesenrad—REE-zen-rahd—giant wheel—GERMAN

Schmaltz—shmahltz—chicken fat—GERMAN, YIDDISH

Shaliah—shah-LEE-ah—emissary—HEBREW

Slečna—SLECH-nah—Miss—CZECH and SLOVAK

Talmud—TAL-mood—body of Jewish civil and religious law—HEBREW

Torah—TOHR-ah—the Pentateuch; the sacred text of Jewish law and teaching—HEBREW

Učitel—UCH-it-yel—teacher—CZECH and SLOVAK

UNO—The United Nations Organization

USSR—Union of Soviet Socialist Republics

White Papers—decrees the British government issued restricting Jewish immigration to Palestine

Yeshivah—yuh-SHEE-vuh—institution of Jewish learning—HEBREW